TOOLS *of the* EARTH

TOOLS *of the* EARTH

The Practice and Pleasure of Gardening

JEFF TAYLOR

PHOTOGRAPHS BY
RICH IWASAKI

CHRONICLE BOOKS
SAN FRANCISCO

FOR JOY AND SERENITY, AND FOR XP

Text copyright © 1998 by Jeff Taylor.
Photographs copyright © 1998 by Rich Iwasaki.

Library of Congress Cataloging-in-Publication Data available.

ISBN 0-8118-1909-4

Printed in Hong Kong.

Design: Jane Elizabeth Brown

Distributed in Canada by Raincoast Books
8680 Cambie Street
Vancouver, British Columbia V6P 6M9

10 9 8 7 6 5 4 3 2 1

Chronicle Books
85 Second Street
San Francisco, California 94105

www.chroniclebooks.com

ACKNOWLEDGMENTS

GARDENING IS A SOLITARY PURSUIT, BUT WITHOUT THE WISDOM AND ASSISTANCE OF OTHER, MUCH BETTER GARDENERS, THE AUTHOR WOULD HAVE DESPAIRED MANY TIMES. GRATITUDE IS DUE IN BIG BUSHEL BASKETS, ESPECIALLY TO MY FAMILY: TO JOY, MY LIFE PARTNER AND WISE GARDENER; TO SERENITY, OUR DAUGHTER; TO MY MOTHER, HAZEL, WHO PICKS AND PAINTS FLOWERS; AND TO MY BROTHERS JON, TIM, AND THOM, ALL GARDENERS.

THERE HAVE BEEN MANY OTHERS WHO HAVE GIVEN SUPPORT, FRIENDSHIP, AND EN-COURAGEMENT AS THE AUTHOR LEARNED TO GARDEN AND WRITE ABOUT GARDEN-ING, AND HE WISHES TO THANK THEM AS WELL: EWA KOWALSKI, JENNIFER WNUK, AND ALAIN GELBMAN, FOR GREAT ASSISTANCE IN POLISH TRANSLATION; PAT STONE; BONNIE AND BRENDAN CARMODY AND DENNIS AND LIZ WILLIAMS, WHOSE GARDENS REFRESH THE SOUL; IKE AND MARY IWASAKI, WHO GENEROUSLY MADE THEIR GARDEN AND GARDEN TOOLS AVAILABLE FOR THIS BOOK; ROGER RICHARDSON AND JERRY CAMPBELL, WHO BROUGHT MY COMPUTER OUT OF COMA; VICI NOTEMAN, FOR THAT DELICIOUS RECIPE FOR ZUCCHINI BARS, AND HER HUSBAND RUSS, FOR TAKING ME UP IN HIS PLANE SO I COULD GET ANOTHER PERSPECTIVE ON OUR GARDEN.

SPECIAL THANKS TO KATE CHYNOWETH, MY EDITOR AND LIFELINE AT CHRONICLE BOOKS.

TO THE SPIRIT OF GARDENS EVERYWHERE, THE GREEN MAN. MY DEEPEST THANKS TO HIM.

CONTENTS

INTRODUCTION

If the study of carpentry taught me how ignorant I was in youth, gardening has revealed the amazing scope of it and lengthened the journey of knowledge into middle age. Every season has been like the first grade. But after years, now I can grow a tomato. That was my original, my *only* goal in becoming a student of gardening.

About fifteen years ago, I was the thing that garden expert and author Steve Solomon calls a "corn and tomato gardener," skimming the top of the garden without diving into its real mysteries. Exploring them can take a lifetime. I am still only an experienced amateur.

As such, I've discovered there are millions of gardeners and millions of gardens, and no two are alike. There are also many reasons to garden. Some are practical, some philosophical, and some are clearly spiritual.

If you believe in such things as a soul, a garden is said to be good for it, but the proverb that there are no atheists in gardens may not be true. A garden is made of mundane things, dirt and seeds and sweat, and people who doubt the existence of numinous phenomena can still grow carrots and corn. But once they step into a garden, they have to wonder how flowers grow and vegetables ripen, and even the most hardened doubters become halfway persuaded that Something is going on. They may fight it, convinced that a garden is nothing more than germ plasm responding to external stimuli. They may think that loving the earth and working with its intelligence are irrational concepts. It doesn't really matter; they ultimately find their own secular peace. Gardens improve the mind, flooding the brain with oxygen and challenges, raising a thousand unanswerable questions about subtler realms than this one.

Gardening is an act of love. When you raise a single flower from a seed and it becomes a luminous red tomato that drops in your hand like a gift, you can easily fall in love with the earth. Love means work. It is a lifelong commitment, since you are temporary and the earth is permanent; it's not like you can threaten to leave. The new gardener's honeymoon lasts until the first weed, blight, or drought. Then it's time to work on the relationship.

My co-gardener and life partner, Joy, usually understands when my efforts are unsuccessful, and why. She has a connection with the earth that I cannot fathom, and a love for plants that keeps them a deep green. In gardening, I humbly follow her lead. She is the sheriff of our garden, a born gardener. I have seen her resurrect a dead stick into a flowering tree. She has watched me do the reverse. One learns, in love, to listen.

About eight years ago, we began gardening a section of our pasture, which slopes gently down the hill all the way to the river. It was hardpan mixed with gravel. Where the back lawn stopped, the old pasture began; for years, horses had eaten the life out of the soil, and by walking the fence like convicts, eventually they trod the surface into a clay tile floor called *laterite*.

By adding horse and chicken manure, and with Joy's careful management, we've reaped increasingly better harvests each year. It feels, some days, like a monstrous pain in the kazoo, but at other times as if we are personally saving a tiny corner of the planet by increasing its biodiversity. We have fresh mint, fennel, squash, potatoes, artichokes, butter beans, turnips, Jerusalem artichokes, spinach, cosmos, corn, tomatoes, chard, sunflowers, thyme, peppers, marigolds, anise, eggplant, sweet potatoes, broccoli, asparagus, zinnias, cantaloupe, nasturtiums, blackberries, raspberries, carrots, wild carrots, mustard, wild mustard, dock, dandelion, wild oats, pigweed, and thistle. Our garden is a festival of edible, beautiful, and pernicious plants.

This summer, we pushed the fence farther back to plant corn, reclaiming even more land. For openers, it had to be busted up with picks, mattocks, and spades before it could be tilled into anything resembling soil; fifty years ago, our intended corn patch had been a graveled road leading to a sawmill. On the other hand, the plot had been well littered with horse fertilizer the last thirty years. Mix clods and organics together, add time and tilling, and you've created loam.

The day I moved the fence, which turned out to be a larger enterprise than originally planned, I rose the next morning and had a vision: If every person in the world put the same energy into gardening that he or she spent watching television, the whole world could be a garden again. Gardening is an act of hope, an affirmation of what is possible. Read a newspaper. Then read a seed catalog. Which one makes you feel more hopeful?

These are not the confessions of an expert gardener, but of an average Joe Hoe, driven into a life of subsistence farming by a love for tools, a desire to grow food for our table, and the enthusiasm of my best friend. The right spirit of gardening, she advises, is never goal-oriented. The harvest is not the end of the journey, but the close of another semester, the afterglow of a hard sensual connection.

Gardening is hard work, if done in the right spirit. My understanding of the terms of Adam's sentence is that, running concurrently with sweat of the brow, tilling the earth is also required: work + dirt. Hoeing weeds has taught me that some tasks are their own reward.

With a shovel or rake in hand, the reasons to garden are obvious: one must be industriously tilling the soil, shaping the beds, spreading the mulch, leaning on the pitchfork's long handle, and watching the fertile earth in order to witness its magic trick—a few seeds, a little water, and hey presto, a tomato. Or corn.

My fondness for old tools has been dimmed considerably by the research for this book. The progress made in garden-tool design has taken great jumps in the past few years, and there are hoes available that make the classic garden hoe look like a crude stick. If a high-quality shovel can be ordered from a gardening catalog, there is really no point in using an old one at the end of its life.

The tools we use to garden will not give us peace in themselves. The computer, an excellent gardening tool for the dirt-challenged, can easily harrow peace of mind, so it is merely mentioned and does not warrant its own chapter. This book is about tools that link our hands to the earth, to help the soil perform its miracles, tools to cultivate the rocky ground and make it lush, or to stamp out some flora or fauna that threatens the garden. Tools alone cannot change us. Only hours spent in a garden can do that. Tools provide the excuse to be out there, working.

Gardens are great teachers, not in words but in gentle or stunning lessons. They teach faith and miracles, knowledge and wisdom, hope and sweat. They are also very cheap psychiatrists. This is not a sanity-inducing time in human history. When our psyches reel from the rat race, when traffic is bumper-to-bumper, and the clocks tick like whip-strokes inside our souls, we can take all the crap and manure to our garden and leave it there. We reap perfect serenity of spirit, standing on a green island of peace in what Japanese gardeners call this crowded, speeding, wasteful, motorized civilization: *kotsu-jigoku*, or "transportation hell."

This book is also about a few people who garden. They are not planting gardens to save the planet, but to learn. Much can be learned in a garden that cannot be explained in any book. This one offers several methods to start an experimental compost heap, and suggests tools to seek or avoid, and lists many ways to murder slugs, but such information is the banging of a drum when compared to the lessons your soul will find in a garden, growing like the lilies of the field.

Foremost of these lessons is happiness. This is so little to ask: that one's life be enjoyable. It is a carefully cultivated attitude. Humans have found ways to enjoy their lives, to savor each moment, in the most horrendous places. It behooves us, we who live in developed countries and use three-quarters of the planet's resources, to enjoy our lives to the hilt. Most of our physical needs are covered day to day, and the things we really want are not always and forever out of our reach. We should be grateful that we have so much leisure time to pursue happiness.

In one sense, a garden is only earth consciously modifying itself. Our bodies are made of the same elements found in healthy soil and seawater, so it is nothing short of a homecoming when we touch the earth. Best we should do so reverently, because the earth sustains us.

Gardening is our favorite outdoor hobby. A big 85 percent of Americans are out in the weeds, because otherwise we might go mad. Wars, stock markets, and politics do not exist here. The problems of a garden are real and basic, small matters of life and death to be sure, but nothing you can't fix with a hoe or some bone meal. You can hear yourself think, and if you listen closely, sometimes you can hear the earth speak. It always says, *Tread lightly*.

S H O V E L

All gardens begin with the shovel, or spade: a stick whose blade touches the planet. At the other end, some specimen of humanity is attempting to rearrange the terrain for some worthy purpose. Worthy to humans, at any rate.

If you like to shovel, you'll love to garden.

Today's purpose is worthy enough: I'm going to spread twenty tons of gravel, to establish a path between barn and garden so feet and wheels won't sink into the earth. The drainage ditch, dug last week with a trenching shovel, will get backfilled with crushed rock, in which I have great faith.

It's not a particularly bonny morning, even for January. Winter's menu for today features yesterday's leftovers, a cold and brittle rain. All the rivers are bursting their banks, running just below flood stage. When this valley was covered by solid old-growth forest, it drank up all the sky could send. But that was over a century ago; all the giant trees are gone. Supersaturated, the earth melts into slop.

On the bright side, here I stand in oilskins, holding a shovel and waiting for the second dump truck. A philosopher once wrote: "Only a garden can teach you that nothing is terribly important." A shovel is the perfect tool to accomplish life's meaningless tasks in a meaningful way. Life is either too complicated or brutally simple, but a shovel always works.

The second truck arrives, spraying a bow wave like a motorboat as it brakes on the rainy highway. Smiling down from his nice warm cab, the driver more than slightly resembles the bulldog hood ornament. I point to the spot.

He backs his rig up, bouncing along the tree-arched driveway between barn and house. It's a squeeze, like a dog jumping through a tire swing. The top of his bed barely misses the trees, pruned yesterday just for this trick. Raising the dump,

he avalanches ten more tons of wet two-inch-minus—a term meaning rock crushed to two inches in diameter or smaller—right smack on the stake. His machine looks like a dinosaur, stretching its back. Then he roars off down the highway into the misty forest with my check for two hundred bucks and eternal gratitude.

This is a good-size mountain of gravel: twenty tons of it, a tangible wealth of rock. Now it must be moved and spread. To do this, I have a wheelbarrow, rake, and shovel. While it is a good shovel, with a pretty yellow handle and a lifetime guarantee, it is still only a shovel. A tractor, even an ugly tractor, would be the right tool for this job.

When you plan a strategy of major landscaping, take a good hard look at ways to do it from a sitting position. A tractor combines the functions of at least three garden tools: shovel, wheelbarrow, and Adirondack chair. It is not a mere indulgence but a machine that will pay for itself the first time you avoid a heart attack. On the other hand, working with a shovel is good for the cardiovascular system, and it raises serotonin levels to build strong minds.

Thank God for exercise, then. Our current solar income, to use Paul Hawken's phrase, is a trickle of illumination. Oregon's climate dissolves structures and shuts out sunlight all winter. For weeks at a time, it is like being locked inside a wet, rotting box of a house while serving an endless, colorless sentence. Storms are a nice change, making us almost cozy as they blow in from the west or south to break on the tiny farms in the coastal mountains.

These are old, worn-down mountains, probably a seabed at one time; the raw dirt is either red sticky clay or yellow crumbly clay, and it adheres to shoes, shovels, and tires. Add too much water and you have world-class mud. By stirring in tons of organic material and baking it with sunshine, it can be gardened.

Our garden won't be ready to dig for months. When my grandfather farmed in Iowa, he used to pick up a handful of his own black topsoil in the spring, squeezing it into a ball to determine the tilth, an old term meaning its readiness for sowing. When wet enough, it would adhere for just a moment before crumbling. He always smelled it before letting it fall back to earth. Sometimes he tasted it. I'll bet it tasted like dirt.

Craning skyward, I send the usual short prayer for more good weather and a tractor. In the meantime—and indeed, winter is a very mean time—I have time and a shovel.

TOOLS OF THE EARTH

All the works of humankind, from ancient pueblos to the Eiffel Tower, from the Hanging Gardens of Babylon to the one in our backyard, required the use of this fundamental tool. It's a meditation stick, a baton for manufacturing sweat, an ancient lever for moving earth from one spot on the planet Earth to another, or for turning it over to put in gardens and thereby replace the original flora.

This has been going on for centuries. The Cedars of Lebanon occupy a few square acres in the middle of a desert. The cradle of Western civilization is now an arid, blasted land, but once it was a forest stretching for thousands of miles, the fabled land of milk and honey. Even today, forests are being cut down somewhere to clear land, and shovels dig the foundation for houses made of wood milled from the missing trees.

On the other hand, Rome was once a great civilization, and look at it now. Latin became a dead language shortly after Romans enslaved others to run their shovels, just as our current troubles began when we monkeyed with internal combustion and atomic fire. Things were going fine before that. There's a cheery thought: If I get a tractor, it could be the first step on the road to decline.

The history of the shovel disappears into antiquity, but my personal acquaintance with it has been lifelong: almost half a century of delving gravel, loam, clay, bark chips, manure, snow, grain, sawdust, and hot asphalt. And not a little bit, either; tons, hills, mountains, all moved from one location to another on the crust of the planet, one scoop at a time.

There is something heroic about a person digging with a shovel. Pathetic, maybe, but also optimistic, and definitely the stuff of heroes: an impossible task, an inadequate tool, a lone paladin standing beside a wheelbarrow with the sky whizzing on his head, a modern Sisyphus. There is something absurd about starting our garden in January, too.

Revving my throat and pretending I'm a tractor seems to make the wheelbarrow feel lighter. As long as we're hallucinating, my dream tractor will have a power take-off, creeper gear, and multiple hydraulics for scoops, backhoes, augers, and blades, maybe even a snowplow that I'd never use. We get less than a foot of snow per year, up here in the temperate zone of the coastal mountains. Too bad. If we were snowed in occasionally, a tractor would be an essential, rather than a luxury. A snow shovel kills more of its operators than any of its cousins.

I fill the wheelbarrow with gravel, about 300 pounds of rock, and lift. Six vertebrae pop, with a crunching sound like celery. So this is what gravity on Jupiter feels like. A push forward with my knees to get it started, and soon we're moving downhill in a graceful stagger. Empty, rake out the pile, and repeat. If I were riding a tractor, I'd be yawning by now.

The extended forecast is for increasing drizzles and blanket overcast turning to showers, with possible thunderstorms and sleet throughout the week, which is the long way of saying rain. Winter in Oregon is not to be confused with a Hawaiian vacation. Color it dark gray, and hose it down without letup or surcease until it squishes. On November 17, 1805, Captain Clark (of Lewis and Clark) bitched in his diary that eleven solid days of it had pretty well ruined his opinion of Oregon.

The syndrome known as Seasonal Affective Disorder—early pioneers called it "cabin fever"—is directly linked to light deprivation, which can make a shotgun barrel look tasty. So you make your own sunshine, any way you can. I choose to work with a shovel, and to begin our garden in my mind, and to dream of tractors. I believe in the future. Soon, I'll be able to shovel manure on a hot day.

The shovel in my hand has a fiberglass shaft, which is a bit of an experiment for me. Normally, I favor wood handles. There is no question that the best shovel handles are made of wood. But it should be emphasized that "best" does not mean strongest, just most traditional and hand-friendly. Steel is stronger than wood, but it's far too heavy. Fiberglass is also stronger than wood, lighter than steel, and more waterproof than wood. The only thing is, you must wear gloves because fiberglass handles can inflict blisters the size of dimes. You should wear gloves when you use a wooden-handled shovel, to avoid splinters, but you don't have to.

With a little digging, one can uncover all sorts of facts about the historic role of shovels, not just in constructing civilization but also in the interface of wilderness and human habitat that we call "gardens." The Mesopotamians took certain herbs and flowers from the wildwood and placed them in high terraced beds, to create the Hanging Gardens of Babylon. Even with hydraulic pumps, it must have been a nightmare to water, to say nothing of moving all that soil with shovels and wheelbarrows.

But they were not the first. Gardening was an old pastime even when the Egyptians built formal walled gardens with stunning arched entries, very much like the country gardens of England of five millennia later. The ancient Persians were artists with shovels, shaping rivers to flow in fanning rivulets through vast gardens in and around their cities, where first flowered the study of science: astronomy, mathematics, medicine, and horticulture. Like gardeners today, they looked over the fence occasionally to see what their neighbors were doing. Their word for gardens they envied, *pairidaeza*, gives us our English word, *paradise*. Crusaders brought home Moorish garden architecture, with arches and enclosures, a style that soon spread all over Europe. To the east, Buddha's followers took up shovels and planted sacred groves of trees throughout Asia, from India to China.

From tiny window boxes to commercial truck gardens, a garden is the place where humans can work inside the larger plan of life, encouraging it with a few tools. It is an orderly sort of life, to be sure, and a well-tilled garden is lush in a different way than virgin jungle. In fact, a shovel is the natural enemy of jungles, because it can erase them—for a while. But the jungle always wins, eating phosphates from the ruins of formerly great cities. Working under these conditions, I have a hard time drumming up much hope for civilization.

However, as long as I'm alive and standing in this pelting rain, our little farmstead will endure. We can keep the wilderness pruned back, inviting certain plants to grow on our property where we have dug a home for them. We cause the water to flow around us, by making ditches with a trenching shovel. It's not a tractor, but it's far more reliable.

All shovels, and all spades too, have three parts: the handle, the blade, and the shoulder, which we can call a footrest. A shovel is a lever that will move mountains, but its design also allows the body to rest in a standing position in all weather. Rest often and long, fellow and sister delvers. In use, it's best to take small bites and work slowly, like a sexton. Naturally, I'm wearing gloves, boots, and a sacroiliac brace with suspender straps, since my spine is half a century old and made out of fine porcelain.

After an hour of this brooding and delving, Joy calls me inside for breakfast and a hot towel. Multiple refills of caffeine blow away some of the fog, and with it the tractor fantasy. I won't get done today, or even this week. In fact, as I tell Joy, it will require divine intervention to get that gravel moved, ever.

"Don't worry about it," Joy tells me. "Put it in God's hands." She says that a lot when I get discouraged. She has buckets of faith.

"Tell God I need a tractor," I mutter.

Months pass. Somewhere in there, I get four tons moved, one shovelful at a time. Spring formally begins on the equinox, and it's still raining. Few sights are more hopeless than a person standing beside a slightly dented Matterhorn of gravel, of which sixteen tons remain. Some people say a garden is made out of mud, but a gardener's made of muscle and blood . . .

Once and for all, let us define a shovel and spade, because the words are not synonymous. A shovel has a concave blade, with a tip that is sometimes rounded and sometimes square, and a handle that may or may not be full length. The steel is stamped in a hydraulic press to form the frog, which is the depression under the handle socket. By contrast, a spade has a flatter blade, is also either round or square, and also may have a short D-handle or a long straight one. But observe, the spade's head is sturdier than a shovel. It can be used for cutting sod and, in a pinch, for scooping soil, although the shovel obviously is the better tool for shoveling. In a garden, you'll use both about equally often.

Our spade's head was forged by hand in England from a single chunk of carbon steel, and is frogless, with an actual closed socket for the split-ash D-handle; a Sovereign, by Spear and Jackson. It came paired with a garden fork, the classic hand tool for tilthing, which is beating clods to pieces after a spade has broken the ground.

The first known steel shovel in America was manufactured in 1774 by Captain John Ames of Massachusetts. At one time, American shovels and spades were among the best in the world. Many are still high quality, especially those with fiber-glass handles. But if you find a very old wood-handled spade in good condition, buy it. Behind our barn is a knee-high stack of rusty, dead shovel heads; none of those cheapies lasted one full decade. Our new English spades and antique

American shovels look good for another fifty years.

As I begin to lift more gravel into the wheelbarrow, a dozen generations of delving ancestors come to watch their descendant work, their brawny or scrawny builds reflected in my own muscles. I notice that most of my forebears seem to be leaning on shovels, or spades. In my earliest memory of my father, he is holding a shovel, a tool that goes back in my family to the Potato Famine in Ireland, when Benjamin Isaac Tyler decided to dig bogs elsewhere. Legend says the authorities desired an interview, which he did not, so he changed his name and sailed to the New World.

Once established in America, the newly named Taylors spread out from Boston, delving like maniacs. Taylor is the twelfth most common name in this country, so the Irish tribe easily blended into the larger family, the melting pot theory in action. But show a Taylor a shovel, and if he or she grabs it without thinking, we are probably related.

When my father first let me use a shovel, I was five years old. I had been watching him dig a trench in the California hardpan, and asked if I could help. As my hands touched the warm ash handle, gigabytes of racial memory began to download. I sensed that, in the future, this tool would forever decorate my life.

But I couldn't break the crust of the soil, even by jumping up and down on the shovel's footrest. My dad took over and did it easily. "Practice, son," my father said. "That's all it is, is lots of practice."

I took him at his word. For hours uncounted, I have broken my back by swinging a shovel, moving bites of the planet from one spot to another. In my youth, I was a fast digger, trying to get the excavation out of the way so I could build; instead of taking frequent breaks, I worked faster. Now I have a good shovel and a bad back.

If work is love made visible, as Gibran swears, we might say that shoveling in a garden is sweat in the service of the sacred. Each spade of earth is an offering, sending out a prayer for growth. There are times when working a shovel can be misery made manifest, but for the most part, it's all leisure time in a garden. You can think, pray, reflect, or meditate while shoveling. The lessons keep coming.

So do the days of sunshine. In mid-May, when the soil is finally dry enough, Joy calls around until she finds someone who can till it with a tractor. He comes out one Saturday and finishes the whole job in two hours. "Long as I'm here," the man says, eyeing the mountain of crushed rock, "do you want me to spread that gravel?" Which he does, in about ten minutes. He won't take any extra money for it. From Joy, I get one of Those Looks.

A week later, I am double-digging a new bed, taking the first bite of soil with my garden spade, drinking in the birdsong and feeble sunlight, when the brevity of it all strikes me. In particular, the human season seems pathetically short, a flicker of breath and water in motion, a blip of life in the eons of eternity. Nothing I do will last forever. I am brother to the shovel, which moves earth from here to there without changing much of anything. Someday, this tool will evaporate back into the elements from whence it came, just like my body and soul. Consciousness doesn't tarry long in one body. It's a sobering thought.

But then I ponder the Miracle of the Moved Rock. Brief or not, my life has been touched by magic more than once. I resolve to pay more attention to each passing moment, and always to dig a little deeper. Given a few years and a good shovel, or a spade, a limited consciousness housed in a fragile body can accomplish miracles. Awareness is a tool, also.

**Save on the rare occasions when the sun is shining,
I am only here for fun.**

◆

HILAIRE BELLOC

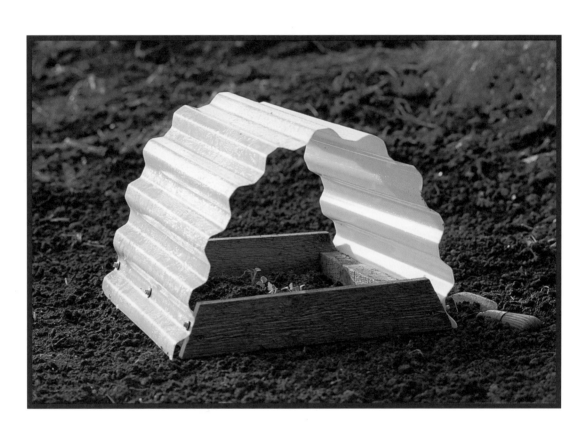

C L O C H E

There can be no doubt that spring is here, except for the fact that it's not. Around the time of the vernal equinox, Oregon likes to take a break from the rain and throw the inhabitants a sun party, with lots of clear skies and balmy air, a few first buds appearing, and the air smelling of fresh green things. There is a light breeze; not the cold slap of winter on the back of the neck, nor the hot honeysuckle wind of summer, but the almost warm breath of counterfeit spring, two months early, to be followed by a rainy intermission lasting from mid-March to late June. Oregon has a beautiful false spring.

Newcomers to this area waste time taking down their storm doors, which they'll just have to put back up again. For seasoned gardeners, this is a precious break, a time to use the good weather to prepare the garden in every way possible except for the actual planting. Today, we'll order a dibble and a trug from Walt Nicke, and oil and sharpen the rest of the tools for this season's garden. For the next two weeks, the days will be completely booked up, spent fighting back the jungle or repairing the rot. We will gather more firewood, break up the soil a little, mow the lawn, and pretend hard that this is going to last, because it won't. Daylight must not be wasted, and every waking hour should be spent nose to the grindstone and forehead to the ground.

But: "We've got to build some cloches today," Joy insists. This is apparently at the top of our ten-item list.

I'm not sure what's going on. Four years ago, I built a greenhouse. On the south wall of our garage, I poured concrete for a slab and built three walls out of studs, with a big picture window of glass in front. The walls were covered with a clear miracle plastic, according to the manufacturer: rigid corrugated plastic that cuts the sun's harmful rays while admitting the beneficial ones. The plant shelves were made of cedar one-by-twos on a stud framework, nice and solid, with a potting

bench on the back wall. Finally, I hung an expensive storm door with a built-in screen, and devised some sliding screened vents on the back wall to keep it cool throughout the summer. Since then, I've installed a ventilation fan for a little extra air movement. I figured that would be the end of it.

It wasn't. Two years ago, in response to Joy's pleas, I built an eight-foot cold frame on the south side of our house, with a lined bottom that would hold a foot of horse manure to heat it up, and a lightweight lid made of the same miracle plastic. A cold frame is basically a box, free-standing or not, with a lid that admits light. Flats of young plants are kept inside a cold frame until they're ready to be planted. With electricity or some other heat source such as rotting manure, it becomes a hot bed.

Over the past four months, Joy has been chanting about the need, the overwhelming urgency of building some cloches, and I've been nodding agreeably, hoping it would pass. It has not. Joy continues: "We really need to get some seedlings in the greenhouse transplanted out in the garden, and we can't do that until they're protected."

I try to wiggle out of it. "What about the cold frame? Can't you use that?"

An hour passes, during which Joy teaches me a short course in the science of early transplanting, the difference between cool season crops and warm season vegetables, and the necessity for "hardening off" some seedlings. We could indeed use the cold frame, she says, and we already are, but it is immovable and set apart from the garden. A cloche, by contrast, is a removable womb that is placed temporarily over transplants out in the garden.

The soil temperature today is a balmy fifty-three degrees. This is a good midpoint, apparently; cool season crops include onions, chard, turnips, lettuce, fava beans, peas, spinach, and a few others. Some of their seeds will germinate at even lower temperatures. Warm season vegetables—tomatoes, peppers, cucumbers, corn, and eggplants, to name a few—need more warmth. You can either wait until the soil warms up past sixty-five degrees, or use a cloche and black garden cloth to make it that warm. Even after hardening off, these wilting violets can't take freezing temperatures. As a fan of tomatoes and peppers, I begin to see the impeccable logic in building cloches.

This year, Joy has been growing hundreds of seeds in tiny fiber pots on our windowsills, putting them in the greenhouse as the weather warmed up. I assumed this was just to get them out of our kitchen, but it wasn't. The idea is to harden them off, giving them a little bit of stress, just enough so their stems will be strong and their little systems used to stronger sunlight, cooler night temperatures, and a tad less water. Transplants from the store or nursery are grown under ideal conditions, and if you put them out in the garden after the last frost date, they still might expire from the stress of cool nights or too much rain.

One advantage of a cloche for tomato growers is an early start on the season. Cloches require a bit of fiddling and fine tuning; during a sunny day, they must be opened for venting, or the heat will build up and fry your little plants.

Joy is ready to put out some seedlings to let them harden off. She's already cut back on the water supply, and if this weather holds, some afternoon this week, she'll move her tiny pots into the new cloche, after I build it.

There are a number of ways to acquire cloches. Simplest of all is buying them commercially. One good reusable cloche is made from clear, flexible plastic tubes filled with water, about a foot and a half high, that encircle and insulate individual plants and still allow venting through the top. Lee Valley of Canada sells them for a little over ten dollars each, but they last a comparatively long time.

Another type of instant cloche-building material, Reemay, is sold in rolls. It is so light that a square yard weighs only slightly over half an ounce, and it can be used as a "floating" row cover, supported by the plants themselves. Laid over seeded rows or transplants, leaving a little slack, it also makes a good bug screen.

A heavier protection of the same kind is a membrane called Gro-Therm, which increases daytime soil temperature even better than Reemay, but is not as effective for frost protection. Someday I want to try both of these.

But for today, I have a few ideas of my own, and will try to invent cloches using materials at hand: a bit of clear corrugated plastic, a roll of six-mil clear poly, a few one-by-fours, four eight-foot lengths of PVC, and a few pieces of plywood.

My first design involves cutting the plywood into four-foot squares, and then using a jigsaw to cut out one giant letter "D" shape from each. It wastes a lot of

plywood, but that can't be helped. When I have four of them made, I link them up, sixteen inches apart, with a bottom framework of one-by-four stock. By covering it with the corrugated plastic bent over the top, this creates a little plastic Quonset hut. Finally, I put copper tubing all along the bottom inside edge, to repel slugs. The conditions inside a cloche are so wonderful for slugs that they come for miles, and one is tempted to use slug poison bait, but only for a moment. The copper will work all right.

Joy raves about this first cloche. It's light and easy for the two of us to move, but it's open at the ends, a small defect I fix with screen to keep out insects. This allows a little air movement, enough for venting, and we can seal both ends off at night with plastic.

My next design is much simpler and cheaper, a temporary quick-and-dirty method because I don't have enough material left to build a cloche like the first one. After Joy has planted a row of lettuce, I bend the four PVC pipes into a letter "U" shape, pushing the ends of the pipe into the ground about two feet apart. It's tricky to get them to line up, and I have to push hard to get them seated. Then I connect them along the top and both ends with duct tape, to stiffen them up a bit. I cover the framework with the clear sheet poly, using duct tape at the bottoms of the pipe to hold it. It's little more than a tent, not very elegant, but it works.

Finally, I make up one little tiny cloche by bending the last scrap of corrugated plastic over a frame. I figure that's the end of it. But once again, I'm mistaken.

"You know," Joy muses, "we could use another cold frame or two, and I'd like to have more cloches like the first one you built. Four or five ought to be enough. Come September, we can plant more greens and have a late winter harvest. And it wouldn't hurt for us to have a hot bed someplace, with electric heat. We could use some propagators, too. And could you make some more of those tiny cloches for next year?"

What do women want?

♦

SIGMUND FREUD

TILLER

The Metal Mule

On this red-letter day in May, the sun has managed to beat back the clouds, and while the soil is still a bit soggy, we may never get a better chance to till our garden. This break in the weather will last less than a week. June is often a wet month, perfect for watering the new plants and seeds, but not so good for tilling and late in the growing season to boot.

Right now, the tilth is almost perfect. When I pick up a handful of turned earth and squeeze it lightly, an act as old as cultivation, the soil holds the impression of my hand for just a moment, and then it falls apart. Today would be ideal for tilling, but it isn't going to happen.

"Nope," Joy says, hanging up the phone. "There isn't a tiller to be had anywhere." She's called around, and every tiller at every rental shop is booked for weeks. This year, we've decided to plow up the earth ourselves, partly because last year's tractor man is unavailable.

I spend the day double-digging and breaking up sod with a potato fork. It's something to do, and it will help the earth dry out. By working from dawn to dusk, I get most of it turned over.

But the next morning dawns, and our original problem is unsolved. The sky remains a bright blue; the sun is still cooperating. If anything, the soil is even better for tilling than yesterday. Plan B: Joy starts calling neighbors and relatives who own tillers.

"No good," she says, hanging up the phone after hours of dialing. "Dave is using his tiller today, and Chester's going to borrow it tomorrow, and somebody else has dibs on it the next day. Dolly's not home, the Dudley-Tucci's sold theirs last year, and Django says his won't start."

Say what you like about technology; in terms of labor, the difference between double-digging an entire garden and running a tiller through it is profound. A

good tiller is nothing short of wonderful in its ability to turn the soil from a hard, clay-based, water-glued plaster coating into a creamy moist brown granulate you can shape to your heart's desire.

Use a cheap tiller first if you want the full effect of comparison, before you get behind the reins of a top-notch machine. One year, we rented an Ariens, the first time I'd ever touched one, and its operation was so intuitive that I felt like an expert after ten minutes. The year before, we used a relative's rented Troy-Bilt; he insisted, and we were glad. It was, as he said, an excellent machine. Over the collective years of our gardening, Joy and I have tried out a number of tillers: the time-tested Gravely's, a Mainline BCS, and a John Deere, all top-quality, full-size machines. Twenty-five years ago, I was privileged to use a Howard Rotavator, the Rolls-Royce of garden tillers, made in England and priced accordingly. But I have never used an actual Rototiller, the brand that gave them all a generic name.

Since we can't locate one today, we now have the option of buying our own tiller. This does not displease me at all. During breakfast, Joy and I discuss the various ways to juggle our economy, and soon we have almost talked ourselves into the possibility.

"Can we afford a new one?" Not that either of us would buy another old funky tiller, for any price.

"Only if we can find one for three hundred dollars," comments the Secretary of Finance. And thus we go shopping for tillers, but only new tillers. No antiques, and let me tell you why, from the beginning.

In October of 1962, I knew I was going to love the sixth grade. For one thing, we got to go under our desks, cover our eyes, and remain there for five minutes, waiting to be vaporized. We also watched a movie with a catchy jingle performed by a baritone quartet who sang, "Don't be a shadow and a pile of ash, Drop and cover when you see the flash!" Best of all, we were released early one day and told to go straight home. Our principal solemnly called it a "special emergency drill," and since it meant a half-day off, it was an improvement on ordinary fire drills. We all fervently hoped it would become a regular event.

As Russian warships drew closer to the American naval blockade around Cuba, our teachers began ducking out in the middle of class for a smoke, puffing like

fiends in the teacher's lounge. The phrase "civil defense" kept cropping up, conjuring up images of armed partisans sniping Russian invaders at the beachhead. For two incredible weeks, the air was thick with tension and nicotine fumes. My parents not only smoked more, they took the unbelievable step of buying a gasoline tiller.

Both born in the Midwest, Mac and Hazel had not a single agricultural bone left, apparently the result of childhoods spent laboring on farms during the Depression. There was much I did not understand about adult behavior, but seeing them sit at the kitchen table and plan their first backyard garden, I knew that the world was upside-down. "We'll need a tiller," Mac said. "We plow up the garden now, fertilize, and plant in the spring." They made a list, which included live chickens, chemical fertilizer, seeds, buckets, a new shovel, and a rifle.

In the thick of the Cuban Missile Crisis, when the television ran all day and night to monitor air-raid warnings, the Beast appeared in the yard, under the basketball hoop. It was old, used, gray, oily, basic, and front-tined. It was nothing more than two handles made of steel pipe, a caged frame for the one-piston engine, and a throttle, all of which sat on a row of swastika-shaped crooked bars, a nest of tines that were supposed to whirl around at low speeds and churn up earth.

The motor started with the aid of a cotton rope that came entirely free with each pull, similar to the first outboard motors. My three brothers and I watched as our dad gave it a mighty pull. For half an hour, he gave it a series of mighty pulls, muttering darkly. Finally the engine popped into life, and the gardening began.

But not for long. When Mac pulled the throttle, the tines bounced and scrabbled across the ratty lawn, and he was dragged along for a respectable distance before he shut it down. After several tries, the tiller finally dug in and churned down a few inches. For five minutes, it operated perfectly. Then it quit.

It is fortunate that World War Three did not start then.

Neither did the tiller after that first time, which was its last mistake. My father had an unusual relationship with small motors and could persuade most of them to work, but this one had the cooperative spirit of a dead mule; though Mac wound and pulled for hours, nothing happened. His face lost all expression, and then tightened. At one point, he took a deep, ragged breath and spoke an amazing, multi-adjectived phrase, the last compound word of which described a barnyard perversion that none of us had ever once imagined as a possibility.

Mac wound the cord around the flywheel one final time, and gave it a pull, without effect. Perhaps it was flooded, or it may have suffered internal injuries from the kick he gave it, right after the rope whipped off and the knot struck him in the cheek just below the eye. I looked at my brothers. We knew it was doomed even before he fetched his tool of last resort, a ball-peen hammer, to make sure none would ever again mistake this inbred, pockmarked chicken-violator—I am paraphrasing, for his language was much more robust—mistake it for a working piece of machinery, such as a garden tiller.

It was apparent we would starve if forced to garden. That same day, Mac bought a .22 rifle, explaining that we could loot canned food from grocery stores, if need be.

We practiced target-shooting for hours, which is great fun if you are ten years old. It was explained to me, first in school and later at home, that if our family survived radiation poisoning, we would have to hunt, gather, glean, or grow everything we ate. Civilization would collapse, but gardeners would prosper. I remember my mother's words—"Farmers never starve"—and that my parents bought two goats. But the Russians blinked, and Mac hauled the tiller wreckage to the dump, and the goats disappeared, and life went on.

The next spring, I started a garden with a little shovel and a rake, planting only radishes. It was my first gardening experience. For one season in my childhood, I grew and ate my own food; some of it, anyway. I still love radishes, but the taste of one always brings back a smell of cordite and vague, paranoid images.

In 1986, Joy and I bought our first tiller, used but supposedly functional and only fifty bucks. It looked ominously familiar to me. In fact, it was the same model of machine that had beaten my dad.

We lived in the city then. Our house had two lots, and we turned one of them into a garden, after I rented a tiller. Suffice it to say that the Son of the Beast's performance was unsatisfactory. It may not have had syphilis, it might not have been forged of ore mined from the bottommost circle of Hell, it was probably not sentient and evil, but it put me through a trial similar to my father's, although I lacked his ability to describe it. So I cannot recommend purchasing an antique tiller for

the beginning gardener, the expert gardener, a stranger on the street, or anyone else but a blood enemy.

Whether to buy or rent a tiller is an intensely personal decision, and you should consider how often you'll need one. Personally, I'd been ready to buy one for years, because we live thirty miles from the nearest rental place. I'd have bought two, just to have a spare. Theoretically, we could have mortgaged the house and bought five, and thereby made a killing in the tiller-rental business, since they're always in demand when spring comes.

This was how we came to own a Mantis, a budget tiller for a small garden. It's well named, as the engine somewhat resembles the head of a praying mantis, and the two upthrust handles complete the image. Because we plan to expand the garden, we're still thinking about a big tiller someday (with reservations, since there are philosophical issues involved). But the Mantis is also good for fast cultivating between rows, as we found out, which means it can be used all season. A big tiller, on the other hand, might get used only three or four times a year, if that.

The first and only hitch we encountered with our little machine was that it didn't seem to till deep enough—but I had put the two tine-wheels on the wrong way, for cultivating instead of tilling. Switching them around solved that, and our tiller fluffed up the ground nicely. The Mantis has two cotter pins on the drive shaft for changing and cleaning the tines, and if we have any criticism, it would be the cotter pins. They take some getting used to.

It's a bit small for tilling up our large garden, but handy for light cultivating and weeding, soil conditioning and aeration, trimming beds and plowing under compost; best of all, it's light and small enough to use in the raised beds. It cost about three hundred dollars, whereas the big rear-tine tillers we fancied ran five or six or eight times that.

If there's any con to the pro-filled issue of garden tillers, big or small, it would be the fact that they run on fossil fuels. This means that they're noisy, but that's easily solved by wearing hearing protection. But by using any gas-operated tiller, we are adding a little more pollution to plague the world. With our own hands, we put noxious carbon compounds to the air, and help to deplete the planet's limited oil reserves. Not to mention the energy it took to build our cute little tiller in the first place.

I don't know if there's an answer. We already drive a car and a pickup, own a lawn-mower and chainsaw. We use electricity like it was water; I'm writing these words on a computer hooked up to a giant salmon-killing dam. As long as we're part of society, enjoying its fruits and benefits, we'll have to face our own contribution to its ills and evils. There aren't many good alternatives to a motorized tiller.

The only consolation is that, by using this machine, we're growing our own food and improving the soil. Our decision not to buy a leaf-blower, a shredder, a hedge trimmer, or an eater of weeds helps assuage the guilt. We're making fewer unnecessary trips in our vehicles now, directly because we have added another gasoline engine to our lives.

To be truthful, I'm not at all sure we could even garden without a tiller, or that we would want to.

Everyone is always in favor of general economy and particular expenditure.

◆

ANTHONY EDEN

G A R D E N
T R O W E L

Joy in Mudville

This is a true love story. It's about pain and patience, soil and serenity, dibbles and dreams, mysteries and miracles. Spanning a continent and almost twenty years, flouting all sorts of impossibilities, it should begin in a garden.

On a day in 1983, a monk filled a clay vessel with some soil from a sacred rose garden in California, scooping it up with a garden trowel. He mailed it up to Oregon, and then he walked back into the garden to work. Perhaps he prayed for an increase in the sum total of human love and happiness; that the jar would arrive safely; and that the soil, wherever it was cast, might bring forth. He picked up his garden trowel, brushed off the dirt with his hand, and put it away.

Fast forward to the present: In our garden, sometimes in the compost pile, often in her greenhouse, occasionally underfoot, Joy keeps her favorite planting tool. She seldom puts it back on her potting bench because she intends to use it right away. Then night falls.

One thing that makes it such a convenient tool is that someone else always brings it out of the rain, wipes it dry, oils it, and puts it away. She must think it's the work of garden fairies. But it's only me.

This English-style garden trowel was made before either of us were born. Joy likes it because it is hand-friendly, although recently she has been eyeballing the newest plastic hand trowel in the Walt Nicke catalog, a bright yellow wonder called the Handform. It's ergonomic. It's lightweight. It's made of plastic, called "polycarbonate engineering resin," apparently because it's a damn good grade of plastic, and rust-proof to boot. "We should buy one of these," Joy said last week.

For now, she uses her equally sturdy True Temper trowel, a phrase that cannot be repeated rapidly without coming apart; but let me add that this company manufactures good tools that do not come apart easily, and they're available at reasonable prices in most garden supply stores. Anyway, Joy's trowel is shaped like the cutest

little shovel, barely a foot long including the stubby wooden handle. Refer to the picture in this chapter; does it look classic, or plastic? You should see its clean lines when it's sticking out of a burlap sack of potting soil, or riding in a bucket when Joy is side-dressing plants with bone meal or compost.

Her method of making plants from seed entails starting them early. About the first of March, little sprouts in brown pots begin to crowd our windowsills. The greenhouse gets a thorough cleaning with a hose and light disinfecting with half a cup of bleach in five gallons of water, splashed wildly about with a broom, because fungus is the death of seedlings.

Joy does all of the planting. Touching the earth comes as naturally to her as plowing it up with a motorized tiller does to me. It's not that I lack any plant-nurturing instincts, but something about spending a day in the greenhouse separating hundreds of seedlings, all the while working dirt deep under my fingernails, makes me severely claustrophobic. Taking those buds outside and grubbing in the dirt on my knees is equally unappealing; the chance to get mud caked on my big clumsy hands knocks me out like an hour in a dress shop. To hold up my end, I spend that day working at the fringe of the garden with long-handled or gas-operated tools. Or writing in the hammock.

By stark contrast, Joy loves this elbow-deep involvement with the soil. She starts right after breakfast, smiling like a giddy earth mother, for this is the Superbowl Sunday of born gardeners, the few days after the guaranteed last frost. The cold frame door swings up, the greenhouse windows crank open, and the dirty work begins without me. But she is not alone; all her gardening friends are doing the same thing. They coordinate it by telephone and confirm it at the general store. No doubt her women's circle discusses the pending magic day of transplanting. Throughout the community, garden trowels dip into fresh dirt and potting soil, making little beds in the earth. They gently backfill tiny root balls, tamping them in with little love pats. There is much actual hand/dirt contact because most of them don't wear gloves. The garden trowel minimizes it, at least.

The name "trowel" comes from the French *truelle*, which in turn derives from a Latin word, *trulla*, meaning a small spoon or ladle. The trowel is always complemented in its work by a hand, which gets very dirty if planting is done correctly.

When you find the right garden trowel, take it to your bosom and cherish it forever, meaning put it away after use. You might favor the modern fluted design or the traditional English transplanting trowel, or rely on an aluminum-alloy dibble to plant your seedlings. You might want its handle to be made of wood, rubber, or composite plastic grip. These are personal choices.

Choose well. This is the tool you'll use to show the earth, mother of all your molecules, how much you care. Think of it as a tool of love; and no, I'm not being overly lyrical, but allegorical. The best love stories always begin with pain and wind up with joy, with the lovers enduring all sorts of travail between the harrowing and the harvest.

Speaking of pain, the earth is kind but not always foot-friendly. Therefore, in addition to gloves, I usually wear lace-ups or rubber Wellingtons whenever I step outdoors. Just today, I picked a huge piece of glass out of our corn patch, an archaeological footnote from a time when a sawmill road ran through it a century ago. I have sprained my ankles and dropped bricks on my feet while wearing sandals, and I have stubbed my toes and stepped on broken glass or dog manure while walking barefoot. High, military-issue waterproof combat boots with steel toes and Vibram soles protect feet from such nonsense, and to my way of thinking, a prudent person should always go shod thus. A beach is a safe place to go barefoot, and Japanese teahouses, but not a garden.

This is demonstrated anew when I let down my lifelong guard and go sauntering through the backyard in Birkenstocks to turn on the hose. The one time I am careless enough to leave my favorite toes unprotected, I locate Joy's gardening trowel with the big toe of my right foot, slamming into it at the end of a pace as if I'd kicked it on purpose. My sock does not immediately start dripping red, so apparently the toenail is still attached. For a while, I have to hop around on one leg, spitting out synonyms for fertilizer.

This is a fortunate discovery. The trowel is almost a foot long, made of shaped steel and turned wood set into a socket. Magnificently designed, evolved from the original triangular mason's trowel and now fully adapted to the garden, it's a beautiful old antique, still dirty from the last use, and until my toe found it, also lost and abandoned. If you don't take care of your goddarned gardening tools and hang them back up on the potting bench, they will rot, rust, vanish, or stub unwary toes.

Assigning blame is easy, because it's Joy's trowel, the one she hasn't been able to find.

I take the gardening trowel into my shop (which is a real mess today, but at least everything's under cover, not lurking under nasturtiums). Lips buckled tight, I knock off the dirt with a steel brush, and rub the handle and blade with an oily rag. Breaking off a piece of my mind and wrapping it in recriminations, I go looking for Joy.

There she is, kneeling beside a tomato seedling and carefully cradling it into its new bed of soil. The new sunlight streams down on her hair as she brushes a wisp of it off her cheek, leaving a smear of dirt. At this angle, it hits me all over again; she's beautiful, in her green rubber gardening clogs and Slug Festival T-shirt. A few more wrinkles, a little more Joy, but I am no longer the Tarzan she married fifteen years ago. After all that time, her face is still serene.

I limp away, cooling down some more, not yet in the right mood to give her back her trowel. What bothers us most in others, including and especially the ones we love, is usually a reflection of our own unfaced problems. I'm the one who's disorganized; my shop is Exhibit A, and there are others. Joy labels everything in the kitchen and greenhouse, and pays the bills with meticulous bookkeeping. So one forgotten trowel is not a pattern of sloppiness.

Just to be doing something else, I recall how we met, and that means consciously recalling it: always a good exercise, gentle reader, when you are annoyed with your beloved life partner.

In the fall of 1980, I was unemployed, thirty years old, single, with three months' income in the bank and a cat for company. Although I didn't know it, I was about to enter a long winter of discontent. At one point, I wrote a will and braced for my own death.

On the plus side, there were miles of beach to walk and weeks of free time to write. I had decided this was going to be my new life work. In a fit of October skin-molting, I had moved, without any logical reason, to the small artist's community of Cannon Beach, Oregon. There I rented a cabin with a fireplace, and for hours sat staring at the sea in front of a crackling fire and my dumb Underwood. Travel and the ocean air had made three of the right-hand keys sticky: Y, O, and J.

Winter was coming on. One cold morning, walking aimlessly on the beach, I looked up and saw a woman who was strolling the other way. She was barefoot in the surf.

In a sudden, senseless flash of inspiration, I asked her a question about the incoming tide; she didn't know, but we talked for a while. Her name was Joy. She said she was just passing through town, traveling and taking the long way back to her home in Vermont. It was a short meeting, but very pleasant.

In November, I walked the beach from sunrise to sunset, hoping to run into her. Sometimes I took off my shoes. It got colder.

In December, when I had given up and no longer walked on the beach, I saw her on a street. She was leaving town, so I scrawled my address on a sheet of notepaper and gave it to her. She said she was going to be on the road a long time. And then she vanished.

My previous writer's block was a grain of salt compared to this new pyramid, reaching to the moon and touching both horizons. That night and for many after, I trudged down the squeaking sand at land's end, thinking, *Idiot, idiot, idiot.* Small soft waves hissed on the beach, rolling up the sand to kiss my toes and whisper, *You are, yesss.*

At the time, I did not altogether believe in signs and wonders, let alone in miracles. Do you believe in love at first sight? Neither did I, except just this once.

For two years, my life stood on tiptoe. I moved inland. I built houses and read books and took long walks. I tended my own lonely gardens. Finally, Joy wrote to say she was coming out to Oregon in the late fall, and was I busy?

On Valentine's Day, 1983, we were married on a covered bridge a few miles from here. We exchanged our vows while standing on a little patch of soil, sent from a sacred rose garden in Encinitas where Luther Burbank once walked, the humble earth sprinkled over rough-hewn boards from a clay jar. My brother Thom had arranged that. A year later, our daughter, Serenity, was born at home. And we lived happily ever after.

That was the first summer we began gardening together. I was never a born gardener, but Joy was. In Vermont, she cultivated any available patch of earth, even if they were only window boxes. In the dead of winter, our house fills up with schefflera, sansevieria, dieffenbachia, dracaena, ficus, philodendron, wandering jew, jade, palm, cactus, and spider plants. Over the years, Joy has been my teacher. The garden, she says, has been hers.

Okay, I'm ready to give her the trowel now. Joy is opening another bed with her bare hands, tenderly cupping her baby plants. Am I going to stride up and give her a resounding lecture on proper tool maintenance, care, and storage? I am not: "Sweetheart. Guess what I found?" Biting my lip to keep stray comments from sneaking out.

You'd think I'd brought her a chest full of pearls, festooned in orchids. She has been looking for this trowel. She does not smother me in kisses or caress my face with her dirty hands, but instead suggests we go indoors to celebrate with a cup of mint tea. She's the most inwardly tranquil person I know.

"This has been a busy season," Joy says, brushing dirt off her knees.

"Hasn't it, though. I wish we could get away someplace. Just the two of us."

"That would be nice," she murmurs. "We could call up some bed and breakfast in Hawaii and say, 'Book us, Danno.'" We've never been to Hawaii. Maybe we'll go someday.

On the back deck, I trip and stagger slightly.

"Is there something wrong with your foot?" Joy asks.

Biting my lip first: "What? No, it's these damn Birkenstocks. I think they're making my arches flat."

> . . . the love that consists in this, that two solitudes
> protect and touch and greet each other.

RILKE

WHEELBARROW

Five Legs and
a Wheel

In the science of simple machines, there
are three kinds of levers, cleverly called levers of the first, second, and third kind.
Although you might not think of it that way, a wheelbarrow is a lever of the
second kind—fulcrum at one end, effort at the other, and the weight in the middle. This lever works on the same formula as all other levers: effort multiplied by
its distance from the fulcrum equals weight multiplied by its distance from the
fulcrum. You probably don't need to write that down, but consider: all moving
parts of any purely mechanical device can be reduced to levers, either in principle or structure. The whole world is built upon levers, by levers.

The addition of a wheel makes it possible to move a load as well as lift it. With
this mechanical advantage, you can raise tremendous loads and take them anywhere, even right down a sidewalk in the heart of New York, up a flight of stairs,
into a small elevator with a folding metal door, and thence up to the roof. It is
terrifying, but it can be done.

Atop a brownstone of New York City (as we call it out West), somewhere in
Brooklyn or Manhattan or Queens or the Bronx or other borough, there is a
rooftop garden. This country mouse could not find it again from a standing start
in the Port Authority, since I was absolutely lost that day—Whatsun, Oregon,
has one general store with a pickle barrel and a hitching post—and I had to
follow my host, a seasoned city rat. We had filled the back of his pickup with
topsoil somewhere in New Jersey or Connecticut and driven into the city. He
pushed one wheelbarrow full of dirt; I was piloting another. We rolled on for
blocks, weaving through well-dressed crowds of urbanites. No one even glanced
at us.

A bit of wheelbarrow advice: When entering an elevator with a load of topsoil,
go straight in. That way, you can reach behind to the button for the top floor,
and back out when the doors open. Two wheelbarrows will not fit.

The elevator ride was so hair-raising I've repressed it, except for occasional night-mares of falling, but I remember my friend's garden perfectly, and can almost smell it now: the loamy wet tang of freshly turned earth, mixed with wisps of diesel and the scorched smell of hot brick. Past the edge, just as many pigeons were flying below this garden-in-the-sky as were flapping overhead. I remember dozens of raised beds three feet tall, built over a thin layer of pea gravel for drainage. On a central wood framework against a brick wall, a few tools were neatly racked: spade, garden trowel, rake, and secateurs were there, just like ours back home but of top quality, and a small black wheelbarrow stood on its nose nearby. A city hose, fat and gray as a rub-ber snake, coiled at the base of a serious brass spigot jutting from the wall. There was even a teak potting bench fitted into an alcove beside a telephone, where the city gardener could clip fresh flowers while talking on the telephone, and never get muddy shoes. Gracing a niche was a black stone statue of St. Fiacre, the patron saint of gardeners, brought back from Ireland.

An eruption of flowers and vegetables poured out of other wooden troughs spaced all along the brick parapet, a living rainbow of purple, red, yellow, and green life slopping over the ramparts. In the center bin, I saw a kudzu plant or twenty; their owner, my friend explained, intended to raise them as overnight apartment jungles, and to sell them at an immense profit. The kudzu grower was borrowing garden space in this tiny, tiny cooperative patch of verdant earth that floated between side-walk and stratosphere.

My host asked if I'd pick some tomatoes for the salad, and went inside to start cooking. There are a million stories in New York, and all of them seem to be built vertically. I have always dreaded heights, especially above hard surfaces like streets and sidewalks. But the living fact of two perfect tomatoes, hanging like the breasts of Demeter over the edge, beckoned me to the brink. I traveled the last six feet on my hands and knees. Then I reached slowly out into space and started to pluck them, one by one. I had to look down, and became almost delirious with fear. My hand trembled, but I didn't want to drop the tomatoes. Miles below, a cab was parked at the curb, picking up a passenger, who will never know how close he or she was to being spatterdashed by a tomato falling at terminal velocity. The yellow dot pulled away, and I slithered back from the edge.

I have always associated wheelbarrows with acrophobia. On my father's knee, I heard of his early days as a struggling writer in New York, when he took a job as

a laborer to support his writing habit. He was working on the umpteenth floor of some high-rise, where they showed him a little wheelbarrow, like a gardener's barrow built to military specs. It was loaded with bricks, maybe two hundred pounds of them. His job was to take them through a large window opening, across a two-foot-wide plank, and into the building just across the void. That building had a service elevator.

As my dad told it, the wheelbarrow decided to commit suicide; at midpoint, it rocked left and right, overbalanced, and threw itself into the yawning chasm, raining a shower of bricks and barrow on the alley below, barely missing a taxi. The other workers pulled the plank back inside and pried my father loose with crowbars; he was still hugging it, burying the whiskers of his cheek deep in the wood for extra traction. They told him to go home, but he showed up for work the next day, he said. The foreman applauded his courage and fired him thoroughly, to save his life.

Over the years, I've moved a lot of earth as a carpenter and gardener, and learned a little about wheelbarrow maintenance. The wheel bearing must be greased once a year, tricky since most wheelbarrows lack grease nipples, and the axle checked for wobble and alignment. The bed should be washed out after every use and put up on its nose to drain. If the handles are wiped with a rag soaked in linseed oil, and a shot of oil squirted directly on every bolt that pierces wood, you can extend the lifespan of all the wooden parts of a wheelbarrow, which are the first to break.

When pushing a wheelbarrow, try to keep your shins safely back from the undercarriage; it's easy to bonk them when the wheel catches on anything at all and the barrow suddenly stops.

Once, a wheelbarrow helped me to attain a short but glorious state of free flight. In Colorado, I thought to move some rocks out of a garden patch by wheeling them down an extremely steep hill. Since gravity was on my side, I brainlessly overloaded the wheelbarrow with rocks. Never overload a wheelbarrow; it's hard on the handles and dangerous for the operator's back. It started rolling downhill too fast, and I was running behind it when the nosewheel dropped into a ditch; both handles flipped me over the top like a ballista (a lever of the first kind). I cleared the barrow easily and vaulted head-first down the mountainside.

Subjectively, a long time passed after lift-off. Knowing I was probably going to be killed, I composed myself enough to enjoy the sensation of floating along and taking in a beautiful view of the Rockies; I rejoiced in the sweet smell of columbine blossoms and the pleasant breeze of flying. Impact wasn't painless, but I survived, so it was worth it.

Little wonder, then, that using a wheelbarrow sometimes makes me feel a bit airsick.

We have four wheelbarrows. One has been cannibalized for parts and is no longer assembled. The oldest, an antique made of steel right down to the wheel, has become a planter. A big red contractor's wheelbarrow with a plastic bed does most of the work, but our stubby brown wedding-gift barrow seems to be the easiest to roll. Only the bed remains of the original stock parts, and I've modified it to the extent of mounting extension grips above the original handles, so I don't have to bend so far to raise it.

At sunset, my friend, his wife, and I sat in that aerial garden watching city lights come on; I was thinking about the hopelessness of gardening this way. Tilling the soil meant hopping up on the perimeter troughs, garden on the left and a lethal freefall to the right, to delve the contained soil with a potato fork. It was difficult to find many cultivars that liked smog; fertilizing it organically meant smuggling in sacks of manure and peat moss; the soil required scientific watering, my friend told me, and would dry out at the drop of a pigeon-dropping. "It took us two years to get it really established. But fresh salad, picked five minutes before you eat it: that's worth something."

They had made mistakes in the early days, and they no longer put flower pots on the edge of the roof because pigeons kept knocking them off to shatter on the sidewalk below. Their garden was wonderful, an artificial oasis straining to grow in the center of several square miles of asphalt, concrete, iron, and brick. Under the blazing sun of noon in the city, simmering in heat, every plant depended entirely on human hands for its next drink of water.

This was a baby jungle in the middle of a larger, sterile concrete jungle. It is the nature of living things to expand beyond their confines, to go outward. Cut off from everything, how could it ever escape?

A pigeon flapped overhead, spotted the human scarecrows, and pootered off. I had my answer. Even if this garden died, some of the seeds would survive, their germ plasm spattering statues in Central Park. With that kind of a beachhead, the garden could spread.

The reverse, it turned out, was true. "Do you have weeds?" I asked.

"Absolutely," my friend's wife said, with an odd look. "Doesn't everybody?"

I sipped my Calvados and smiled, vaguely happy. I thought: *Chaos theory works.*

To escape from New York City, I hailed a cab. On the dash was a hand-painted statuette of St. Fiacre. The driver was talkative and friendly, recently arrived from Jamaica. His name was Simon. I asked him if he was a gardener.

"Haw, nawt here, mon," he chuckled. "Nobody gaar-dins in thee cit-ty, for true." We talked. He did not know that St. Fiacre watched over gardeners, but I did not know St. Fiacre was also the patron of cab drivers in the big city. As we drove to the airport, Simon touched the figurine. "Yah, Sa-a-a-int Focker, mon, he save us from t'ief, save quashie like you when you ride wit' me, yah." He looked up warily through his windshield. "All sor-ta sheet rainin' down in thee cit-ty, ya know?"

God made the country, and man the town.

✦

WILLIAM COWPER

EDGER

At some point in your gardening life, you may encounter a tool that is neither classic nor particularly modern: the edger. With a blade shaped like a flattened half-moon (or Edgar Allan Poe's pendulum), it makes tidy straight lines of demarcation between lawn and driveway, cutting through sod and soil. Depending on your personality, you may need one tomorrow, already own several, or not know what they are.

Little test here: Is your sock drawer organized? Then you probably own an edger. Is it organized by color? You definitely own an edger, maybe two. Do you clean behind your refrigerator on a weekly basis? You own one hand edger and a motorized edger. Both are in perfect condition.

If, on the other hand, you have struggled along in your master landscaping plan so far without an edger, don't run out and buy one. Give it some thought first. This seemingly innocuous tool could organize whole sections of your life, and not necessarily for the better.

One Saturday morning, Joy and I are shopping at a garage sale in a sunny, upscale neighborhood of Mootown, the nearest big city. The house seems primly expensive and indecently well kept, as do the owners, middle-aged suburbanites as beautiful as Ken and Barbie, if not quite fresh out of the box. Their lawn would shame a putting green. The garage floor gleams like a hospital tray, and I'd really like to get a look at the tools they're not selling, but a rope across the door keeps out the riffraff customers.

And the sale itself . . . a spectacle of military organization, with every item not only priced but stickered with color-coded tracking numbers. Every item has been cleaned, oiled, categorized, labeled, and displayed. I feel shabby just standing here. I drop my eyes; my socks match. Wish I'd shaved, at least.

For sale, there are three types of garden edgers, with prices written on square tags in a precise hand. The first edging tool is a cheapie, a barely used wheelie-bob from

a garden supply store. I don't even want to touch it. And here's a motorized edger, with a cutting wheel made of stiff steel wires. In operation, they whip around at multiple RPMs and saw a neat slot right up against the sidewalk where the rubber wheels roll along. I used one like it in years past, on a landscaping crew in college. A steal at twenty bucks.

But the third is quite lovely and fairly old, a well-used edger that may have been made at the turn of the last century, German made. Thirty bucks, reflecting its antique value. It might have belonged to Manfred Richthofen. Before I know it, it's in my hand. Over at the card-table checkout, the owners of this mansion cast a cold eye on me.

Joy comes alongside. "Remind me to tell you what Mrs. Stepford over there said to me," she says from the back of her throat, without moving her lips. She notes the three edgers, including the old sweetie in my hand. "Think about the edger they're *keeping*." Then she sees my eyes. "Aw, honey, no, put it back—we don't *need* an edger."

I want to buy it; darned if I don't. But maybe damned if I do. When I take my hands off the old wood, the fever of acquisition subsides. Joy is correct: we don't need an edger, even such a pretty antique. It implies an orderliness that may not fit into our lifestyle. My obsessive-compulsive disorder, acquiring hand tools I may never use, doesn't require feeding. We use a spade when we need anything edged, sliced, trimmed, or bordered. True, the edger is yet another tool, more precisely suited for edging. As a so-called authority on garden tools, I've claimed in print that gardeners can always use another tool. This is an exception to the rule, and it proves the corollary: gardeners can always do without at least one tool.

Instead, we take a spatula, some books, and an unopened box of nails to the checkout. The proprietor, Garage-Sale Ken, takes the cash without comment. "Nice day for flying," I remark. One of his eyebrows rises, exactly like a roosting hawk stretches one wing. "Are you a pilot?" he asks, obviously hoping I'm not in the brotherhood.

Negative. No, my passions include gardening, carpentry, and examining patterns, even if they appear unrelated, to see if they fit the profile. So far, the data are inconclusive; but sure enough, it turns out he's a retired fighter jock.

Buying an edger should mean that one wants a landscape with clear definitions, which is reasonable. Use string to plant seeds and your rows will be easier to weed; label plants and you won't have to guess what's coming up. But owning an edging tool can lead into mind-reeling realms of order. I believe that the very concept of owning an edger is probably unhealthy. The desire to impose order, like any other strong impulse, is just a flew blinks away from insanity. As F. Scott Fitzgerald wrote, pull your chair up to the edge of the precipice and I'll tell you a story.

Long ago, in Colorado, my parents had a neighbor whose yard and garden was tended with a vigilance bordering on monomania. Let's call him Mr. Marko. If a leaf fell on his lawn in the middle of the night, it would be whisked into the compost before dawn. His lawn was not just neat and tidy; it was meticulously perfect, with every blade of grass the same shade, thickness, species, and length.

Needless to say, Mr. Marko owned an edging tool. I had several opportunities to watch him in action, carefully separating the surface area of his landscape into lawn, sidewalk, garden, shrubs, and parking. Perfect circles of mounded mulch surrounded his trees. His lawn came screeching to a stop at the garden line, which was marked by pure black loam that he raked every day. So the grass went racing off in the other direction, and this time halted at the driveway in a line only somewhat wavier than a violin string.

One time I caught him whipping his garden into shape, and we talked over the fence; I asked him, with a wonderfully straight face, what the edging tool in his hand was for.

"It's for chopping off the sod, when it grows over the sidewalk, you know? Dividing things. Besides—" he scanned his perfect yard, and then my parents' rambling landscape. "How else do you know where the lawn ends and the garden begins?" This was his answer. All the tiny wheels inside his head ran in shiny grooves, perpetually balanced.

But I envied his organization. His garden tools were color-coded and inventoried, he kept moist potting soil and amendments (bone meal, fertilizer, potash) in numbered plastic drums, and his entire garden ticked through the seasons in clockwork perfection, dying, resurrecting, and flourishing on schedule. His quest for order had been woven into the fabric of his life, which made me feel somewhat better about commercial flying; he was an aircraft mechanic for a major airline. To him, a leaf on a morning lawn was not an artistic touch, but FOD, a flight-mechanic acronym for "foreign object debris."

Still, one lousy leaf? It was not as if a cat were going to trip over it. Watching Mr. Marko pounce on his grass at dawn, still clad in pajamas, to nab one leaf and scan the offending tree for signs of more littering—yes, it was entertaining, but no, it was not a picture of blooming mental health.

Joy and I don't own an edger, have never owned an edger, and you can guess our future plans, edger-wise. The tool for this chapter will have to be borrowed for the photograph. Our lawn dives right into the garden and keeps going, leaving a raggedy edge that climbs up onto the lawn. Grass spills over our concrete in green waves. If it gets too invasive, we might take a spade to it, but otherwise, the jungle is barely impeded.

It's all right, though, to want more order in a garden. Ours would be greatly improved by a cruciform pathway of brick pavers, with high box beds raised and defined by planks, like Mr. Marko's garden. I'd go that far. No edgers needed, though.

In the sixties, one of my uncles owned an edger. He was a jet pilot and didn't garden when I knew him because he was overseas, actively engaged in concealment-denial defoliation of the Vietnam jungles. But his backyard, back in the World, was well manicured, with lawn up to the edge of the green grass, a concrete patio, and bark mulch around every tree. Gray meant concrete. Green meant grass. Brown meant trees or plants. There was no overlap.

In those days of my youth, I had a job on campus. One of my duties was to use a motorized edger to define where sidewalks ended or the lawn began, depending on point of view. Recall that in the sixties, voices were just beginning to speak out against the imposition of too much human order on the natural world. Even my girlfriend asked if I realized the futility of being a tiny cog in the vast running-dog imperialist system. "Your labor is wasted," she intoned, "keeping The Man's sidewalks neat." As a gesture of solidarity with the counterculture and to ensure that the fruits of free love would keep coming, I left a few sidewalks shaggy.

An edger is a good tool for keeping plant life off the edge of a sidewalk. You command it to grow here, and up to here, but never over this line, and the grass will conform.

For a while. You could make a case for grass being a very artificial ground cover; so separating it from the concrete would be completely natural, in a structured land-scape.

But I was beginning to see some fraying around the edges of the American dream. I mowed, I edged, I listened and watched.

I worked at a Catholic college, set like a jewel on a golden hill overlooking a small city. It was run by an order of Franciscan nuns. One day, the head groundskeeper was asked by a delegation of sisters to resolve a problem regarding the interface of Nature and the Divine, to wit: Pigeons were befouling the statue of St. Francis. It was an honor and a privilege for novices to scrub the statue, he was told, but then the disgusting skyrats would just return the next day and paint the saint of Assisi again. Slowly, they broached the subject of pigeon bait. Poison.

The groundskeeper, a devout and plainspoken man, nodded thoughtfully, although his face turned very ruddy. He waited to speak until they had finished. "Sisters," he said loud and clear, hiding nothing from God, "if we poisoned those little birds, I do believe St. Francis himself would shit a brick up in Heaven. Pardon my French." Nuns blinked rapidly, the suggestion was dropped, and the matter forever closed and forgotten.

The next time I used an edger, I was landscaping one weekend outside a closed con-vent of Carmelites, who lived in a walled enclosure on a high knoll out in the mid-dle of nowhere. The groundskeeper had brought me along, a special mark of favor given only to those he trusted, he said. "These sisters like their privacy," he said. I wondered why he picked me, but I was getting paid overtime. My duty was to es-tablish a stopping point for the ring of lawn around the brick bastions. The grounds were encircled by a brushy jungle of thick green plants, clipped into a rude privacy hedge. It was volunteer marijuana, which grows wild all over the Midwest, escapees from the Missouri hemp farms of World War II. "See what I mean?" my boss said on the drive back. It seemed prudent to keep quiet about it, and I have until now, almost thirty years later.

A plain spade will cut a fairly straight line, but an edger can make an absolutely straight line, especially if it's guided by a nylon cord stretched around four stakes. Measure the diagonals so they're equal, and the garden will not be out of square.

A laser transit would also work. But who would want such geometric lines? What kind of mind would seek such clear distinctions?

My inchoate theory: I think it's associated somehow with altitude, real or metaphorical, the special domain of those who watch the distinctions between land and sky, or earth and Heaven. Obviously, these are important distinctions to pilots and priests. A moment's inattention, and flight can instantly become "descent into terrain," as the FAA calls a plane crash; metal wants to return to earth, and only vigilance keeps it aloft. Those who serve God must always try to keep the sacred and profane apart, even while fighting all the other divisions among the flock. You seldom see churches without immaculate landscaping, including edged lawns. You'll never see an Air Force base with sloppy ground cover.

More anecdotal evidence: Go to any military base where military personnel and their dependents are allowed to plant a community garden, such as the aptly named Coast Guarden at the U.S. Coast Guard station in Eureka. You will certainly see the handiwork of edging tools, since sloppiness in certain environments is intolerable. By the way, the tools in the USCG toolshed are all painted white, with an orange stripe, including the edgers.

There's the flight thing, again. Helicopters float over that Coast Guard base. Everyone wears a FOD bag on their belts because they don't want little bits of debris blown up into the rotors from the downdraft on landing or takeoff. Order reigns because it must. Lives are at stake.

There is a place for perfect order. For the rest of us, earthbound, a smidgen or two of garden untidiness proclaims, like the single purposely mistied knot in a Persian rug, that only Allah can create perfection.

Heaven is under our feet as well as over our heads.

◆

THOREAU

H O E

Weeding, it has been said, is the essence of good gardening. The definition of "weed" is an easy one to grasp: Any unwanted plant in the garden is a weed. It may be an edible potherb that Euell Gibbons found delicious, or it may be as toxic as hemlock or poison ivy, or even a volunteer in the wrong place, but once designated "weed," you want it out. In order to cultivate plants of the desired type, all competitors must be removed by force, and often. In theory, you could weed whenever you felt like it, but once tall weeds get the upper hand, making themselves at home among your vegetables, they will own your garden.

Mulch can be laid to smother them, but this presents its own problems, such as providing a nice moist hiding place for slugs or keeping the ground from thawing after the last freeze. Cover crops between the rows are another way to keep the weed incursion down to acceptable levels. But even with these countermeasures, there will still be weeds to hoe—ragweed, hawkweed, bindweed, mayweed, pigweed, milkweed, and chickweed—because the process of weeding brings up more buried weed seeds. Once they are anywhere near the surface, they sprout.

Even plants grown on purpose can become weeds, if they go where they are not supposed to. Take comfrey, for instance. An immigrant herb that was probably brought over from England, it's salutary for chickens, horses, and people, curing nearly everything from ulcers to broken bones, according to herbalists. I find it difficult to call it a weed because I'm so fond of it.

But comfrey is one of those spreading plants. No matter how often you cut the leaves, ten more will spring up. To cultivate comfrey, plant it in a stainless-steel pot about two feet in diameter, with plenty of drainage. Put this pot in the middle of a ten-foot circle of concrete, such as a helicopter landing pad; for those gardening in the Dakotas, a used Titan missile silo works well. If you don't have access to one, defoliate a ten-foot patch of buffer earth between your comfrey and

everything else, using rock salt and Agent Orange to sterilize the zone, and for good measure, sprinkle on a little plutonium dust.

Anything less will be ineffective, and you will have comfrey spreading beyond your wildest expectations, even into your garden, where it must be treated as a weed. And quickly.

For those interested, each weed has its own two-part Latin name and a common one or three. *Cirsium arvense* goes by Canadian thistle, and *Capsella bursa-pastoris* will answer to Shepherd's Purse, but *Verbascum thapsus* is known as mullein and also Aaron's Rod. If you have the stomach for learning these, go ahead. Any name you call them will suffice, so when in doubt, I make them up and save all sorts of trouble: false potato, creeping strangler, glueweed, buggerweed, hoebane, dorkweed, lying mustard, Fescue-Jack, and thistledie.

One of the worst weeds in our pasture and garden is called redroot pigweed, although I have a better and more vulgar name. Grab it by the stem to pull it out and you'll make the acquaintance of a weed that has learned to send a taproot down to the center of the earth. Yanking harder is out of the question; the gristle of your spine will pop loose first, long before the pigweed lets go. It, and all other deep-rooted invaders, must be hoed to death, their stems cut below the soil line and bodies flung into the wheelbarrow. A week later, when it sticks its ugly head up again, you decapitate it once more.

With a long-handled hoe, you shuffle along and kill everything in your path. If you see a slug, the hoe whips out and bisects it even before you make a choice. The tool pulls you down the row, its sharp snout hunting weeds.

I consider myself the best weeder I can be, a quiet affirmation that makes the job more fun. All my attention focuses on the job. When I hoe a weed, killing's my business and business is good. I flip it aside with a snort; mess with the best, die like the rest.

It's not fishing for marlin off the Florida Keys, but I like it. Weeding can be done standing up, zipping them off at the root with back erect and proud, or it can be done in the kneeling position, more tenderly and with greater precision. Joy's method is less hoe-dependent. She would rather kneel beside a tomato plant and scratch or pick out the weeds right up to the tomato stem. For years, she's used an Ideal Weeder, as the Walt Nicke catalog dubs it. The narrow blade is bent into a squarish U-shape, sharpened on both sides and the tip, and set into a hardwood handle. It's also called a hot-bed weeder or a hoe knife, and because of the hook shape, it's ideal indeed for cleaning the stem-fouled propeller tines of our Mantis tiller.

Gardeners tend to get attached to their favorite close-weeding tools. It's partly due to the types of weeds prevalent in given areas, and partly the type of soil, but to a degree, it's also a matter of personal style and brand loyalty. Some prefer a minia-ture mattock called a "Gold Digger," that looks like an ice axe with wicked-looking pointy tines on the back of its head. It can be used to break up extremely hard and stony soil, or flipped over to rip out weeds. Some like the stubby Gardener's Pick made by Snow & Nealley Company, a tool that can reduce the meanest soil to com-pliant loam. Some get by with a rugged and reliable Japanese soil knife, which is exactly what it sounds like: a plain old knife in a plain old sheath. But the *hori hori* is one secret of Japanese gardens, which are close to the pinnacle of good gardening. In practiced hands, one soil knife is tool enough.

Joy has so many close-weeders that she can misplace three and still have lots from which to choose. Her favorite weeder/cultivator seems to change every spring, when Ren and I buy her many new garden tools. For many years, my gardening mentor used only a hot bed weeder to dig, weed, make furrows, and thin rows. Now she uses others, including the Magic Weeder with its three springy tines that scratch out small weeds. The long-handled version of this, Joy discovered, not only weeds but works well for picking apples from high branches. She also raves about the Bar Harbor hoe knife, which is basically a short metal rod terminating in a knife blade turned sideways; it can remove a single blade of grass or topple a three-foot thistle.

I seem to have acquired something called a Trake, an aluminum all-purpose tool with a trowel at one end and a cultivator on the other. Extremely light, it would be ideal for handicapped gardeners. Its rubber grip is so ingeniously contoured that it feels natural and comfortable in both positions, a neat ergonomic trick. Joy gave it to me, on condition that I throw away my old weeding tool.

Some gardeners pick one hand weeder and doggedly stick to it for the dumbest possible reason: simply because it's an antique. My (formerly) favorite one-hand

weeder is an antique, which looks like a miniature potato hook. Since I seldom used it, it spent a lot of time on a shelf of our garden bench. That's what made it my favorite hand-weeder; I could admire its beauty and utility, without feeling compelled to use it a lot. But now I use my Trake, and am beginning to get the hang of close weeding.

The hoe was probably the second tool invented for gardening, right after the shovel. With this long-handled tool, you weed in the upright position, only somewhat "bowed by the weight of centuries." Edwin Markham's famous poem, "The Man With the Hoe," gives us some idea how the world regards the subsistence peasant farmer: "The emptiness of ages in his face," for openers. O. Henry referred to the poem as "those rollicking lines of that merry jingle," but he was being facetious. Its tone throughout is an endless journey of despair, and it comes home with a few unanswerable questions.

Before you pick up a hoe, you should really read the whole thing. It reveals a farmer standing on a blasted heath, his universe as blank as his mind, his dreams akin to the thought processes of cattle ("stunned and stolid as the ox"). It gets worse when the poet asks the deadly question: "Whose breath blew out the light within this brain?"

Finally, to paraphrase the closing poser: If God made that creature and called it Man, this dumb and dull-witted quintessence of dust, what will happen "after the silence of centuries" to kings and kingdoms when he finally goes after them with the business end of his hoe, for the crime of stealing his humanity? This was the thrust of the poem.

I see it in a different light. Clearly, this poor agrarian has been using a dull, misshapen hoe for generations. Even the weeds whip him, after the Cossacks are done. Quite naturally, the result is one badly demoralized gardener. But give this man a decent hoe with a really sharp blade and a long enough handle, and watch a slow smile break over that wrinkled face. It may not be as entertaining as television nor as pleasurable as sex, but weeding with a good hoe can be relatively blissful.

Conversely, weeding with a bad hoe creates the sort of result Markham described. Weeding is an endless task at best, but without the right tool, it is brute labor. Read the work of Barry Commoner, Gene Logsdon, Paul Hawken, or Roger Swain, all expert gardeners and distinguished writers, and you'll see that humans working with a hoe can be simultaneously cultivating the field of contemplative thought, if their hoes are light, sharp, and efficient.

The intelligent gardener will likewise search for ways to make weed management easier because at the end of a day of bending and pulling, chopping and hacking, you will intuit that a few days of this can break your spirit like a twig, and do your body no good whatsoever.

When Joy and I first started gardening together, we went down to the local hardware store and bought a complete set of tools for our garden: shovel, garden fork, bucket, rake, hoe, and scratch weeder. At the end of the first season, only the rake, bucket, and scratch weeder were still around. I had broken the shovel while prying up what I thought was a root, but which turned out to be a buried steel pipe. The thin metal of my toy shovel began to crimp at the frog, even before the handle broke. The hand weeder was completely inadequate, a basic three-pronged cultivator unfit for weeding. (It is still unfit.) The hoe handle was considerate enough to snap near the head, so Joy was able to saw it off and continue using it as a close weeder.

But I wanted a real hoe. At an antique store, I found an old Warren hoe with an arrowhead-shaped blade, supposedly made in Canada at an old-fashioned forge. The handle was too short, but of such rare patina that I couldn't make myself replace it. It was awkward and heavy but nonetheless sturdy, and I used it for many years in the name of tradition and thrift. Of course, weed-chopping always made my arms sore clear up to the earlobes, but I thought that was what hoes were supposed to do.

A little research cleared that up. A hoe is *not* supposed to chop weeds. Chopping is what a machete or a hatchet does; a good hoe should *slice* weeds, like a Ginsu knife.

First, this means a hoe must be sharp; not just pretty sharp, as with the painted bevel-edge you find on hardware-store tools, but incredibly, fantastically, molecule-cleaving sharp, the blade first shaped with a file and then honed for an hour or so with a whetstone. To hold an edge, a hoe should be made of good high-carbon steel. It should be fitted with a handle that is long, strong, light, comfortable, and above all, firmly connected to the head. Weeds will fear such a hoe, which cuts them off

below grade effortlessly so even if they try to grow back from their evil beginnings underground, the hoe keeps slicing off above-ground growth until the roots starve.

Most hoes aren't sharp enough, but in addition, the angle of attack is wrong. Take a look at your own hoe; is its head basically perpendicular to the handle? If so, that means you have to chop down to cut a weed. For modifying standard hoes, you can bend the head to a steeper angle, so that when you're addressing a weed with the hoe in your hand, the entire blade is parallel to the ground. But this involves some blacksmith work, heating and shaping the head without losing the steel's temper, and since cheap hoes will neither bend without breaking nor keep a sharp edge afterward, the best option is not to buy them in the first place.

Gardeners love catalogs like borers love sweet corn. A hundred dollars can vanish in a twinkling; the prices are not necessarily higher than in the mall, but the quality is nearly always better. You will discard the hoe your sainted grandmother left you, once the boxes start arriving from Smith & Hawken, Langenbach, Gardener's Supply Company of Vermont, and Garden Tools of Maine. In search of the Perfect Hoe, Joy and I have found two more garden-supply companies we like, Earthmade and Walt Nicke. The first is based in Indiana, the second in Massachusetts; both sell quality tools and garden equipment and guarantee their products, not to mention our satisfaction. After years of thinking that weeding meant pain and struggle, I found a few great hoes in the above-mentioned catalogs, tried them, and was converted. So I put my foreign Warren in the shed, Fred, and that's it hanging on the hook.

Speaking of slow intelligence, I have used the phrase "stupid weeds" for so long that I seldom separate the words anymore. Killing them with a hoe makes one contemplate their bright, brief existence, terminated with a stroke of my hoe.

I would not presume to question Nature's motive in putting the damned thing in my garden, nor do I believe the weed has no consciousness whatever. Maybe it thinks loftier thoughts than I ever will; maybe weeds are smart enough to survive in a hostile environment because a weed cannot conceive the idea of any environment being hostile. Drop a seed on rocky soil, and you have a perfectly happy weed, no complaints. Try that with a tomato, and usually you have no, or a dead, tomato.

Some random things I didn't know about weeds, condensed from the original ten volumes of my botanical ignorance: (1) Weeds are either annuals or perennials; mulch controls the first class, but not the second. Some perennials, such as perfidious quackgrass, cannot be controlled short of digging up your entire garden and sifting it through your fingers, looking for its rhizomes. Rhizomes are underground stems. Stolons are runners aboveground. (2) If you weed when the plants are wet, it can spread disease. If you weed when the plants are dry but you have been smoking tobacco, it definitely will spread disease—tomatoes are very susceptible to tobacco mosaic virus, but weeds aren't. (3) Many weeds, like pigweed, dandelion, and mullein, are immigrants, unknown to this land before Columbus. (4) Weed seeds are hellishly long-lived; ancient lupine seeds found in the Yukon were still viable after at least ten centuries of burial in permafrost. Ergo, the old maxim, "One year's seeds mean seven years weeds" is far too optimistic; weed seeds can live a thousand freaking years.

I make it a point to admire weeds for their tenacity, their vitality, and their patience, sometimes actually speaking aloud: "Well, aren't you the healthy one. Having a pretty good day, are you?" Then I kill them.

Besides sublimating a lot of unhealthy ambient rage (a common symptom of the nineties), you can make weeding a happy diversion, not unlike a dance: spot a weed, step forward, slice, twist or shake hoe to flip weed, step forward. This rumba can be done to radio music, perhaps, but sometimes I find myself humming as I weed, which also works. Rhythm is the main thing.

My first dance with a hoe came when I was sixteen. We had just moved back to Iowa, and I hoed beans on a farm all that first summer. The rows extended beyond the farthest flat horizon, billions of acres of weedy soybeans. My hoe was an L-shaped blade on the end of a two-foot stick, handmade by the hundreds at a local welding shop: a "bean knife." Its only virtue was that it was very sharp. I cut my shin to the bone in the first hour of hoeing, which would not have happened with a long enough handle. It was heavy-duty, but very heavy.

Below are some weeding hoes I can recommend, having tried all of them in our garden. But please understand that it is by no means *the* definitive list; when I showed this chapter to a dear neighbor, she took me to task for leaving out the Glide-N-Groom and the gooseneck arrowhead, both of which she has used for

years. I complained that the latter looked like a damn Warren hoe, so she led me out to her impressive garden and demonstrated how beautifully it worked. "And there's nothing wrong with a Warren hoe, either. I saw yours; it was just *old*." The new versions come with aluminum handles, smaller heads, and the gooseneck is another tremendous improvement.

The basic scuffle hoe, also called a Dutch hoe, stirrup hoe, or oscillating hoe, is rapidly becoming my favorite tool, ever since I got a good one from the Earthmade catalog. It's called a Pro-Gardener, and the clad aluminum handle is lightweight but extra-long; I'm several inches over six feet, and finding a tool with a long enough reach was a blessing. In addition, the stirrup shape of the blade slides under short weeds, although its thin blade will sometimes cut the stems of big weeds after stomping them flat.

Joy seems to be bonding with the long-handled Ho-Mi, a design used in Asia since the Bronze Age. Its pointy, tapered blade turns inward at an odd but perfect angle. The handle is wood and comfortably long, about fifty-four inches. Be advised, though: it is shipped dull for safety's sake, and must be sharpened before using. I've filed ours to the keenest bevel, wickedly sharp as a hunting arrow, so the side edges can slice dickory-dock leaves. This weed likes to root itself near corn, but the Ho-Mi's point extracts it without disturbing the shallow corn roots.

Eliot Coleman's Collinear Hoe was first brought to my attention by Pat Stone, the editor of *GreenPrints*. It's a clever modification of an ancient design, made in Switzerland with a replaceable crescent-shaped head that is tilted for maximum ergonomic effect; in other words, you can hold it comfortably like a broom, thumbs pointing up. You wouldn't think that would be comfortable, but many experts fervently claim this is the easiest way to hoe. As Coleman is the author of *The New Organic Gardener*, a classic book on the subject, his invention has many years of applied theory behind it. I've used this hoe once, borrowing it to try it out, but we haven't purchased one yet. This may change next year.

Using the Garden Weasel, one is tempted to think that someone has devised a tool to marry the jobs of weeding and cultivating, which seem to have irreconcilable differences. Revolving dragon's teeth on three discs chew up the soil with each pass, forward and back; while it may not obliterate every weed, it leaves them so tattered that few survive. The Gardevator works the same way, only with more teeth and discs. Both are easily cleaned, reasonably priced, and have long handles. Which is best? Fans of Weasel and Gardevator are extremely brand-loyal, always a good sign of customer satisfaction, but I know one gardener who uses both and says they're about the same, only different.

My only problem with the Gardevator and Weasel might be that they don't get the tall weeds in our garden. But weeds aren't supposed to get tall. For that matter, my stirrup hoe doesn't exactly shine on tall weeding, either. And they kill slugs, which the stirrup hoe won't.

Joy's Ho-Mi kills slugs and rips out tall weeds by the roots, which is something to consider if you tend to put off weeding. It's the oldest design of them all, and maybe it can't be improved upon. But hoes are a personal choice; you have to weigh the fun factor. If you don't enjoy the simple pleasure of hoeing, you'll avoid doing it early, which means you'll have to do it later, and thereby have more and taller weeds, but much less fun.

The human will is a weak thing beside the will of a plant.

◆

LUTHER BURBANK

BUCKET

Down by the biggest compost pile, an old steel bucket is slowly filling with rocks. Its only function is to collect stones thrown up by the tiller, a never-ending process because this garden bed is about 10 percent gravel. We've filled it a hundred times, and will keep filling it with rocks until the bottom falls out. It's something for the bucket to do, since it won't hold water anymore. I don't feel bad for the bucket because there are uglier jobs in this garden.

No garden can get by without a bucket or three. It is among the most versatile, ignored, and generally abused tools. It gets tossed about and dropped, filled with all sorts of unpleasant things, left out in the elements, and is never, ever maintained. All other garden tools get an autumn cleaning and a short rest, but never the old bucket. It hauls ashes from the woodstove to the ash can, and fills up with rain or snow in between.

Sooner or later, rust eats a hole and the bucket no longer holds water. Rather than throw it away, gardeners can cut out the bottom and push it in the earth over a plant for a nifty slug collar. A slug can crawl over a razor blade, but not a bucket lip if you wrap some copper wire around the top. Slugs hate the electric taste of copper, and the very sight of a bucket.

Apart from ice-cream makers and sauna buckets, there aren't many old wooden buckets around. They tend to develop pinholes from tiny wood worms that bore into the perpetually wet bottom. And just to clear up a question you may have about an Appalachian folk song featuring dear Liza and dear William, at one time such a hole was repaired by twisting a hay straw and thrusting it into the wormhole; "use straw," exasperates dear Liza. Water swells straw to make a temporary plug. The song, of course, is laden with double-entendre.

Gardeners will rave about their new hoe or shovel, but none sing praise to the homely bucket; poets are also silent on the humble pail. It's just there. One day,

it's gone, made bottomless by hard work, and you replace it with no sentimentality at all. Made of wood for thousands of years and of galvanized steel for many decades, the modern bucket seems to be trending toward rubber and plastic, two materials that are very nearly invulnerable to all the evils buckets are heir to. But the basic bucket design has forever stayed about the same: a cylindrical vessel holding approximately two gallons, wider at the top than the bottom (or vice versa), with a wire bail for carrying.

Aside from the most common garden use—hauling water—buckets have a hundred other functions. They make good small totes for collecting weeds all summer. They carry bone meal and compost right to the bed for side-dressing. A tool bucket will also port your trowel, dibble, and weed scratch, along with a pair of garden gloves. At harvest time, it's an extra container for gathering corn. Fill buckets with water and you can presoak root balls before transplanting. They're perfect for collecting walnuts, cucumbers, and bulbs. Put a bucket over a garden stake you keep tripping over, and this faithful tool will even protect your toes. As stated, they are kicked and abused until they die.

But there is one final fate for a bucket, the lowest rung on the ladder of utility. We have one steel bucket that is used as a holding pen, a death-row cell, for slugs. We call it, naturally, the Slime Bucket. To get some idea how many slugs live in Oregon, know that there are no bag limits.

On midsummer nights, Joy and I go out with flashlights to intercept slugs on their way to our garden. During daylight hours, we make the same patrol, catching stragglers. After an hour of this roundup, we usually have a gallon or two of mollusks. It raises a question: What does one do with a bucket of slugs?

I went to a seminar called "Ridding the Garden of Slugs and Snails." We do not have a snail problem here because the ecological niche of slimy garden predators is filled with slugs. The instructor was a sweet lady of respectable winters, literally in tennis shoes, but a veteran of the war on slugs. She held up a bucket and a pair of tongs. "This is your first line of defense," she announced. "Hand picking." Fine, I thought, but then what? "Then," she said, with a strange, eager quaver in her voice, "you kill 'em."

For the next hour, she explained how slugs in the garden may be turned into dead or missing slugs. She had studied the matter, and the range of options is unbelievable.

Poison and slug bait were first, of course. But we don't use poison. Not for gophers, not for slugs, not even for flies or fleas; we soak everything in oil of pennyroyal instead. But no poisons. There are alternatives.

Some gardeners have written that they put their catch in a freezer overnight, and then throw them on the compost in the morning. This works, but I see problems: One, we keep food in the freezer, not buckets of slugs, fishing worms, or severed heads. And two, dead slugs are a disgusting compost amendment because they break down into protoplasmic snot. Still, this may be the easiest, simplest way to kill slugs and dispose of their bodies. If we ever try this, we must call it the Big Chill.

There are other methods we *have* tried, offered below as poison-free possibilities to those gardeners plagued by slugs. A few of these choices are karma-free, for those who worry about such things.

A note on that, from the garden journal: "Wasting slugs is mostly a question of how, not whether. Our garden, particularly the corn, has been predated rather heavily this summer by deer, raccoons, rabbits, gophers, and slugs. The last category, mollusks, is so closely related to insects that I have no problem with executing them. Mammals give us pause, followed by a lot of philosophical wrestling. I don't shoot them, but I would like to kick them in the ass. An electric fence is one option. Check cost. Investigate ways to prevent slugs."

For difficult philosophical choices, there is a spectrum of proper response, with Gandhi's principle of total nonviolence to all creatures at one end (*ahimsa),* and Genghis Khan's response at the other (annihilation); kill no living thing intentionally, or kill everything efficiently and immediately. Gandhi's garden would be eaten by the entire nonsentient animal kingdom; Genghis Khan's would be a free-fire killing zone. Most decisions about lethal response are correct, I feel, if they fall somewhere near the midpoint. No gunfire or poison, but also no pangs of guilt about offing slugs, albeit as humanely as possible.

The relationship of gardeners and slugs can be summed up in two words: mortal enemies. "These guys are eating everything," Joy mutters one day, looking around at the damage. She lifts up our trap board and spies one, seizing it in a gloved fist. "Gotcha, you little creep. Say your prayers." It's a safe bet this particular slug is about to have a bad day.

My co-gardener has watered and nurtured the garden all through the summer's heat, so clemency is unlikely. She is also set in her beliefs about slugs; no use telling her that these gooey bugs are a natural part of the Oregon ecology, native to this bioregion. At one time, before I became a serious gardener, I even spoke in their defense. Sure, slugs are often found on half-eaten leaves, I stipulated, but the evidence against them is purely circumstantial.

"Chlorophyll and cellulose is missing," said Joy, always the pragmatist. "I don't care *how* they did it."

Live and let live, was my philosophy. But that was before I found out that chlorophyll was missing off my tomatoes; nearby, slugs were emitting little belches and trying to look casual. After that, I made it my business to study *Limacidae amicus*: our friend, the slug.

Maybe these sticky mollusks were once useful to humankind. When the first cavepersons invented glue, perhaps they turned to slugs for raw material, mashing them up into a paste guaranteed to hold hides against the body. For a really good grip on a spear, hunters could first squish a slug or two. And around the cave, the first vacuum cleaner might have been a slug on a stick, ideal for picking up lint, crumbs, small bones, hair, and other debris.

Joy hands me a fresh victim. "Here," she says. "One for the road." Sometimes I lob slugs out into the middle of the highway. Eventually a logging truck roars by and the slug hitches a ride, so to speak. We call this technique the Black Ice.

There are many, many ways to get rid of slugs. Slug eradication, in fact, makes shooting fish in a barrel look difficult. The extreme slowness of slugs allows gardeners time to designate a victim, go answer the phone, write a few letters, take a nap, watch some TV, and then go back outside to smash them with a shovel before they can turn to flee. But this method (the Shovel Off) is crude, unimaginative, and unnecessarily messy. As the poet Robert Burns wrote, "Wee, sleekit, cowering, timorous beastie / I'll take ma shoovle and make you pastie / But och, the gorps are verra nastie."

There are cleaner methods. I've often dreamed of taking a pail of them out to the Bonneville Salt Flats and launching them off golf tees with a driver: the Sand Trap. One can also sprinkle them with salt (the High-Sodium Die), but be advised that salted slugs make a real production out of shuffling off their mortal coil, and there are also disturbing reports that they only fake their demise, lying there stiff and lifeless as a rake handle until someday reconstituted with rain water, at which time they revive and stagger off.

So I pass along the following hint: if you ever drop one into a can of light oil or kerosene and it somehow survives, don't make it mad, because that's one tough slug. The Oil Change sends ordinary slugs beyond the bourne from which none returneth.

But you have to sleep sometime, and that's when slugs will stage an all-out offensive on your garden. Protecting your plants is not simple or cheap, but you can use a bucket as part of the tactical response. Dig a moat around your entire garden, or smaller trenches encircling individual plants, and pour in buckets of crushed eggshells. You'll have to dry them first, not to mention eating many more eggs in your diet. A more expensive way is to use diatomaceous earth, which are the shells and skeletons of tiny sea creatures. But use agricultural-grade diatomaceous earth; the Shell Game won't work with the stuff used for swimming pools.

Making large or little barriers out of copper tubing is another choice; the chemical interaction of slug slime and copper creates voltage, giving these galloping gastropods a slight shock on the Electric Light Rail.

These methods only repel slugs, who remain at the perimeter, waiting for an opening. Gardeners are not a bloodthirsty lot; all they want is for slugs and snails to go away. Squeamish gardeners can avoid doing the job on slugs, and still be rid of them, if they have nearby caves or sinkholes. An acquaintance of ours gardens on a mountain riddled with mine shafts, one of which is bottomless. He takes slugs from his garden and simply drops them in. None has ever returned from the Long Good-bye.

Another gravity-fed slug remover is a swiftly moving river, preferably rapids. Put each slug on a small cedar shingle, insert this little canoe in the water, wish him bon voyage, and your conscience is clear. If he paddles like heck, he might even survive the Unlucky Pierre.

Predators can keep the slug/snail populations down. If you have ducks, you will not have slugs. The Quack Attack is uniformly lethal, as is the Amphibious Assault

of toads and frogs. They, too, dine on slugs and snails. But you'll have to fence your garden for ducks, so if a slug gets past them and into your garden, it is home free.

Finally, we arrive at the most elegant termination of all, and the most humane. Slugs come for miles to drink from a flat pan filled with three inches of stale beer. The next morning, forty or fifty of them will be inside the pan, looking very mellow if somewhat dead. Slugs have perfected a cure for hangover: the Last Happy Hour.

Have plenty, if it be only beer.

◆

WILLIAM MAKEPAECE THACKERAY

HEDGE SHEARS

The Green Man

Trimming an evergreen is simple and requires little of the artistry needed to shape a beautiful hedge. Our so-called hedge is fifty feet long and twenty feet high, never part of any logical landscape plan. This northern windbreak for our house started out as a row of tiny fir seedlings that my father planted in 1982. There are photos of him watering those spindly trees, his green parrot on one shoulder. Both have since flown away. Then, the trees were not even up to my father's knees. He planted them six feet apart.

The trees have grown into a thick sort-of hedge. Mac planted them directly under the power wires, intending to keep them clipped down to eight feet or so, but that's how it goes. When we bought the house, the trees were barely below the hot wires, and I've kept them from ever touching by frequent clipping with the hedge shears. Over the years, they've gotten more opaque, which was intentional, but they tend to be a little wild at the top, which wasn't.

I don't really know what I'm doing, but I've been doing it for years. These hedge shears are not state-of-the art, but at least they're sharp. One of the blades is serrated, to catch and hold the branches; otherwise they'd slip out. Someone gave this design a lot of thought, never dreaming that someday people would have clippers that run a hundred times as fast. It's uncomfortable to think how much experiential knowledge of the shears has been lost in a short time; the old master gardeners on English country estates, for instance, might have known secrets of hedge cultivation and pruning wisdom that only years of hand-clipping could reveal.

Although I'm generally opposed to tools that make excessive noise, it must be admitted that a motorized shear is faster, more suited to the efficient use of leisure time. I've often been tempted to rent one. For some, the point is to have a hedge and still have time to enjoy it. I've seen what some gardeners can do with electric clippers, and it's fantastic.

With the right tools, you can design a living fence of arborvitae or privet, with sides like a green carpet and a flat top to rest a drink tray upon. For thousands of years, gardeners have pruned hedges into privacy screens, fences, walls, and arches. Topiary is the pinnacle of the hedge-trimmer's art: carving trees and shrubs into shapes that Nature never intended. An expert can carve the living plant into shapes, and I've walked through a yard in Mootown that had an accurately detailed locomotive made of arborvitae, a boxwood buffalo, and a hardy laurel Model T. The artist learned the skill from his grandfather, who learned it from his grandfather. Some things are in the blood.

In the Christmas tree field to the east, migrant workers come every season to sculpt the small trees into tight, perfect cones before market. The sight of other people working is fascinating, especially when they're doing topiary with machetes. Last year I wandered over to practice my Spanish and to drink in the fresh-tangerine smell of clipped evergreens. Afterward, I tried shaping our front hedge with a machete, but it was a massacre; I couldn't get the hang of it, though Lencho and Chepito and Chuy tried to show me how. "You're chopping like an Anglo," Chuy said. "Relax. Pretend you're Mexican." But it takes practice to carve a living tree so precisely. The hedge shears are slow enough for beginners like me. They also make a nice sound, conducive to meditation.

In England, there are hedges that date back before Washington was born. If you want to see hedges that were created with a plan in mind, hedges as deeply considered and solidly built as a Roman road, enter an English garden through an arched doorway in a hedge. There you will find a representation of the architect behind the clipper's art. Look around until you see a bas-relief face, often smiling, features shrouded or almost hidden in leaves that are carved as part of the face. Sometimes they're just called "garden faces," but never named disrespectfully as "masks," because even the most simple-minded can recognize that this is an old, old nature god. If you ask about them, you might get oblique or even evasive answers. No one really knows anything about the old boy, except that no one knows his name, which is revealing in itself, because humans tend to name everything. Quite a few people have met him, which is tricky, since he's not supposed to exist.

Walking in the woods, you notice that you are not alone. You never quite see him, but the shape (you thought you saw, anyway) was that of a person. Look harder, and

it's only leaves and branches, with vines for fingers. Rational mind satisfied, you walk on. A vine puts a hand on your shoulder and then pats you on the head, but it's only a vine.

The Green Man goes back a long way. Scholars have tried to lock him down, but he seems to precede everybody. The Romans put anatomically correct statues of Priapus in their gardens, often with a formidable erection; it's been suggested that the early Christian gardeners decided to keep only the face and lose the rest. But that's improbable. More likely the Romans added a body to the nameless Green Man, and naturally their interest was prurient. I'm glad Rome fell, and so is everybody else.

The Green Man comes to us from ancient folk legend, the books all say, meaning they have no idea. The Druids knew him as the witness for the Earth, a man who walked behind the forest, face masked by oak leaves. When Christianity was taking root, driving the weeds of paganism back, he was incorporated into cathedral architecture. Medieval churches bore carvings of faces encircled by leaves and smiling oddly, usually upon the outer walls; these places were set aside for the Old Gods, but priests did not encourage the memory of their names.

Some say the Green Man is actually Pan, but that opinion is not universally accepted. Whoever he is, he watches over thousands of gardens all over the world. No garden is complete without a Green Man, usually a bas-relief icon made of plaster or wood. Among other things, it is an offering to the weeds that must be killed, since the Green Man is brother to the jungle. We have one, carved out of a madrone branch, that faces the garden. All these images let the wilderness know that we know whose garden this really is. We may sow and cultivate the flowers, picking them in due season or letting them fall; but speaking personally, I lack the wisdom to show a flower how to grow from a seed and turn its face to the sun. Someone else teaches them. It is "our" garden because we belong to it, not the other way around.

I do not remember if I have always believed in plant devas and flower fairies, but I do now. The word *deva* is Sanskrit for "the shining one," corresponding to the angelic powers of Western theology, and the gardeners of Findhorn gave credit to them for massive yields from incredibly poor soil. When trimming this mega-hedge, I sense that something is looking out for its health and well-being, whispering advice in my ear: *Don't cut that. Cut these, if you must.* And I listen, and obey.

Nature cannot be denied. When you clip a branch on a hedge, the plant compensates by growing in another direction, sometimes by sprouting two more branches at the nearest bud node. Trimming hedges into flat or curved shapes is an art. The science of topiary takes years to learn, and more years to accomplish the trick with any one shrub.

It's hard to master the hedge shears, and they're brutally hard on your forearms; the first time you shear, you acquire an instant case of clipper carpal syndrome. With practice, you build up forearms that can squeeze milk out of a golf ball.

What a great tool this giant bush-scissors was: quiet, efficient, requiring skill to use. Then the electric hedge trimmers came along, and like so many others, this tool bites the dust after progress is done with it. Few bother to seek expertise with hedge shears; the elderly don't have the arm strength, and the young don't have the patience.

Fortunately, there are still a few middle-aged Boomer Luddites around. I've been practicing with these hand shears for years, having never owned an electric hedge clipper. I've used those in my youth, of course, but now I am deeply prejudiced against them for reasons I have never fully examined. Still, I can defend my prejudices with proof from the scientific, spiritual, and moral realms. They buzz (electric) or roar (gas); they're inherently dangerous to fingers, and frankly, they're too damned easy.

By contrast, the hedge shears last forever, make a pleasant clipping sound, exercise the upper body, and don't pollute. When the Green Man needs a shave and haircut, I think it should be done consciously, one twig at a time.

The Green Man has been called the god of the garden, but it's more accurate to say he is the link between humankind and the rest of Nature. A Green Man in a garden symbolizes our connection with the mystery of all that biodiversity, of which our own diversity is a tiny part.

A few years ago, I was building a garage for an older couple named Elmer and Flo. Their backyard was completely surrounded by tall hedges of hydrangea, although it might have been dogwood, spirea, photinia, or privet. In those days I didn't pay attention, and now I don't remember.

It must have occurred to Elmer that, like most carpenters, I was lonely and in need of company while I worked; so he clipped and trimmed his hedges with a hand shears while talking nonstop, recounting his life from birth onwards. He was built like a fire hydrant, with a glazed pate and a jaw like a block of granite.

I was pretty much a captive audience, but Elmer was a gifted storyteller, never repeating himself or rambling, although he had some other quirks. After a bit of verbal experimenting, I found that I could prune him back like a hedge, cutting off the conversation when it ran toward uncomfortable topics by pointedly ignoring a comment. Elmer would compensate by branching off on a lush description of some tropical paradise he'd visited or some adventure that had changed him forever.

Elmer was a bigot in recovery. When someone says, "That's how they are," in reference to another race or creed, this is clear evidence of bigotry. But when someone asks, "What do you think about such-and-such?" it means that person is looking for a way out.

At first I had to struggle to concentrate on building, but eventually we found our rhythms of discussion, and then I could listen to him like a radio. There was occasional jarring static, when he came upon some buried fragment of prejudice.

He was fighting it. "I was raised that way," he said once, acknowledging that he'd been trained to hold certain beliefs. Under this early programming was a kinder, gentler, more tolerant Elmer trying to get out. Tolerance was the tone of the time; society itself was changing and growing, not without conflict. His difficulty was that part of him sincerely believed we should all come together, but another part feared change and the growth of individuality.

When he clipped a hedge, he searched out tendrils that had crept beyond the intended shape of his hedge. The fact that his hedge was seeking a shape of its own did not deter. You can see that there is no right or wrong about this; Elmer and the hedge were both acting in accordance with their natures. Both were evolving.

The day came when his daughter brought home her new fiancé, who was Hawaiian. For a while, this rocked his world. But he loved his daughter, and if his own wild beliefs got in the way of her happiness, he intended to snip them off. And he did. They grew back, of course, but he kept clipping. The N-word, which had fallen early and often in our discourse, disappeared from his vocabulary. He was pruning his own speech.

Elmer's garden had a terra-cotta bas-relief Green Man that hung on the garage wall overlooking the flower beds. One day, we were taking a lunch break, and his eye fell on it. "You know about the Green Man? You do? Sometimes I wonder what he is."

I think he meant the question in the larger sense: Who is the Green Man? Why do we put his visage in our gardens, if we don't know? What nameless spirit makes things grow? But something made me say it: "Well, he's probably not Caucasian."

Elmer just looked at me, searching my face to see if I was pulling his chain. "I didn't mean that," he said. But he didn't say anything for a while, chewing on it.

I do not know all the details of my own ethnicity, but enough has been concealed, fudged, evaded and whitewashed, with most of the family history blotted a few generations ago, that my curiosity was aroused.

On my mother's side, all is Danish; no mystery there.

But the paternal fork of the family tree is another thing, and some of the foliage includes horse liberators, anarchists, witches, inventors, Irish Jews, African slaves, possibly one Gypsy, and at least two far-flung tribes of Native Americans. All that blood is watered down severely and intermixed in these veins. The old Elmer would have had a field day: thanks to my ancestors, I can tinker, brood, shoot, dance, remember, and sing. I enter mystical states of muddled clairvoyance or black depression; I could cure a scalp with deer brains and shoplift a horse, if need be.

What I cannot do is make a real hedge. The genes are absent there. What progress has been made thus far on this hedge, the very fact that I haven't killed it yet with my clumsy haircuts, is due to the tolerance of the Green Man, whose love sees no color except green.

Fairyland is nothing but the sunny country of common sense.

◆

G.K. CHESTERTON

PICKUP

Painted Wagon

The aura of an old truck can free your imagination, but the smell of a new truck can derange your mind. The fact that it might as well be parked on the moon, cost-wise, is masked by the musk of the interior: switches and toggles galore, a big winch, CD, CB, electric everything, rides like a boat and drinks fuel like an aircraft carrier. This is not a pickup truck, but what pickups have become: earthbound rocket ships.

The man with the gold rings and silver eyebrows sees me inside this pheromoned cocoon of plastic and chrome. He moseys over to sell it to me, but I'm already out and standing way back. We came here looking for a practical vehicle that will haul supplies for the house and garden, not padded transportation to debtor's prison. It's just a truck.

"Sure is a beauty, isn't she?" No. To my eye, this hairy block of steel looks like a he; there's nothing ladylike or elegant about this behemoth, from the tall knobby tires to the sullen shark-gray paint job. If this truck were a woman, I would not arm-wrestle her for money.

"Out of my range, though." I want a pickup priced somewhere within the pale of sanity, preferably an old classic truck with some history. His name is Wayne, and trucks are his game. During the handshake, he scans me, a quick assessment almost faster than the eye can follow, from tennis shoes to earring hole. "I'll bet we could put you in the truck you *really* want," he insinuates, "and any color, too." He wouldn't believe the pickup I really want, or understand why.

Wayne tempts: "You could even lease it." Way in the back of my brain, I've been thinking about the garlic gold standard, which is a local colloquialism for raising garlic as a home business. Organic garlic is bringing high prices just now, and the number of new antibiotic-resistant plagues seems to be increasing. The new neighbor, for one, seems to be selling all the elephant garlic he can grow. But at this point, the concept of my own garlic plantation is just a dream to chase. At these prices, on foot.

But a warm sense of financial well-being seems to come over me. Using only his eyes, smiling like a fisherman, Wayne somehow conveys his high opinion of my net wealth. Of course I could afford it, by borrowing up to the hilt and beyond.

Wait. We need more debt like slugs need more salt. How does he do that? What a useful talent for sales. He can make motives lock and inhibitions turn aside, and now Wayne senses that I'm teetering. "Let me ask you this," he says, in low hypnotic tones. "If we could sell it to you for the price you want, are you ready to buy it *today*?"

This is a trick question, designed to put a pen in my hand. Fortunately, Joy comes rushing over and pulls me away, toward the used end of the car lot. Wayne is too smart to argue. She has found a small blue Toyota with a friendly aura and good tires. Aura is important with pickup trucks, even more than color or rubber, but never as much as price. It is not a classic, but the price is right, and it has a good motor.

Bill or Bob, a clone of Wayne but less upscale, shows us the engine. It runs, apparently. Without much excitement, we pay cash, sign forms, and take it home. ("Pay as you go," Scott Nearing said.) Someone else wrote that debt is the worst form of poverty, and I'll remember it when this little truck breaks down.

It's possible to garden in the country without a pickup truck. But out here, high in the coastal mountains of Oregon, a pickup is the primary vehicle for many families. From one end of our little community to the other, most of the gardeners have pickups, and most pickup truckers have gardens. Some of those gardens are even called "truck gardens"; on weekends, the whole family delivers fresh fruits and vegetables to farmer's markets in the Valley. One such lady of the soil refers to her vehicle, a rare Volkswagen pickup, as her "garden truck," defining all its duties in the service of growing vegetables. Eyelashes are painted on the headlights, and its aura reeks of patchouli. She drives it to church on Sunday morning and picks up mulch on the way home.

So far, we haven't found anything our little pickup won't carry to or from the garden, but it's too old to be comfortable and too new to be a classic farm pickup. The dash has been recently chewed to rags by the family dog, who somehow locked himself inside on a rainy night. It has a working radio, heater, and seat belts, basic transportation stuff. We are not particularly fond of it, and call it the Pile for short.

Driving this beat-up farm wagon imparts a correspondence with my great-grand-father, Nels Christiansen. He was a farmer in Denmark, of a race of farmers all the way back into prehistory. In a faded yellow photo, he sits stiffly up on his farm wagon with a pipe protruding from a stark black beard, the reins held easy in his lap. The back of his wagon is piled high with something, probably potatoes or barley or oats; two immense horses stand ready to take it to market. His wagon has air-conditioning and power steering, plenty of horsepower, and all of outdoor Denmark for an ashtray. He may have loved his horses, but probably not his wagon.

They say he paid all his debts before leaving the Old World; didn't believe in credit or banks; bought the first pickup truck seen in his county; and died pretty far in the black for a Dakota farmer who barely spoke English. His son-in-law, yet another Dane and my grandfather to boot, bought his pickup for a hundred dol-lars in cash and eggs, and it ran faithfully from before the Depression until after the start of the Vietnam War. Trucks were trucks, in those days.

Our paid-for pickup is a motorized farm wagon, a horseless buckboard. All year long, we haul sacks of bone meal, bags of potting soil, rented tillers, mulch, fer-tilizer, sawdust for the barn, and bales of straw for garden mulch. We sweep out the bed between trips and keep it maintained, but it's not the kind of truck that evokes any warmth or sentiment.

It is, however, useful and practical for gardening. Try fitting a new wheelbarrow or garden cart into the trunk of an ordinary car to bring it home, and you'll dis-cover yet another reason to purchase a pickup. We've transported as many as three wheelbarrows in the back of ours.

The basic vehicle rule is, older trucks break down more often than newer trucks. Unless you have established the kind of rapport normally found only between a peasant and his beloved donkey, your pickup may strand you in an awkward place, such as the midpoint between town and home. Either the engine will mysteriously stop, or the transmission will fail to transmit motive power, or perhaps the only problem will be a flat tire. But the net result will be the end of locomotion.

The Pile's first flat tire happened on the way back from the coast, with a tarped load of shrimp shells and fish guts. The road was narrow and the day was hot. At high speed, the truck had been able to outrun most of the smell and all of the flies. After it flapped to a stop on the narrow shoulder, both caught up.

Hauling this kind of fertilizer was an experiment, never to be repeated. Few garden amendments have the olfactory authority of fish guts. Potential Samaritans would slow down to see if I needed help, but even had they not noticed the blinding whiff coming through their vents, they could not fail to miss the giant fly halo. One by one, they broke eye contact and sped away, retching.

The Pile is an interim pickup, and so far, we haven't bonded with it. A new pickup truck is not a priority and never will be, but wishing is free. If price were no object, I'd look for something really old and classic, a true farm pickup such as the 1951 Chevy. You don't see many. Literally, they don't make them like that anymore. It had a bottom gear so low it could almost plow.

There is a great diversity of old pickups in this community, with a few classics: a 1952 Ford, a 1929 Model AA (Henry Ford's most successful farm vehicle), a 1955 Dodge, and assorted Internationals of rare vintage. In many parts of the country, International held the almost worshipful loyalty of farmers, who claimed their trucks could not be killed. It's easy to fall in love with old trucks. Buzz, a local beekeeper, drives a 1956 Studebaker transtar, immaculate, sky blue finish, original seats, with a chrome searchlight and round pedals. When our neighbors drive such time machines down the hill to Mootown for feed and seed, parking them in front of old storefront cafes of many calendars, they blend right in. Those old farm pickups have been around so long that they are part of the rural milieu.

Sometimes they become part of the rural landscape. Across the river, the skeleton of a 1948 Ford pickup molders back into the earth under a huge maple tree, whose annual mulch of leaves has saved the truck from blackberry vines. It was towed there in 1965 by a farmer on a tractor, which is all that is known about its history. The engine and transmission have been stripped, and all the glass is missing, but the interior looks good. The body is perforated with bullet holes, the doors alone shot more times than Bonnie and Clyde.

I have scavenged for clues. There was an old sickle on the front seat, its handle rotted away and the thin blade completely consumed by rust. In the glove compartment was one leather glove, hard as a stick, and a map of Nevada. Ten copies of *Popular Home Craft* were tucked behind the seat, stiff but still readable and full of stories about the march of technology from October 1937 to June 1942, when "Build a Home Root Cellar" gives way to "Victory Trellis for Your Garden," and the wartime issues have advertisements explaining how you can't buy their product until the War is Won, usually capitalized. Many articles offer ways the average gardener can stop the Axis.

The driver of this pickup smoked Luckies. He may have been a farmer with tall grass, an amateur woodworker, a soldier in the war. That's all I can deduce, except that he used his pickup to raise crops somewhere around here. There was a pitchfork head in the back of the bed, and the remains of a bushel basket that had once held walnuts. There are indecipherable bits of someone's past scattered all over, under this tree, bits of paper too faded to read, feed bills and shopping lists. No names.

This is the truck I really want, in a little better condition. And then I would like an old yellow road leading into a small town that vanished before I was born, where biplanes sputter in the sky overhead, and to park at a little cafe where coffee costs five cents and refills are free. This is the sense that comes of sitting behind the wheel of an old pickup truck, in common with the lure of old things; they are time machines.

Sweet childish days, that were as long as twenty days are now.

◆

WORDSWORTH

GLOVES

The Gauntlet

Human skin is relatively hairless, covered by a paper-thin nonvascular epidermis made of five layers and protected from UV rays by melanin, a dark amorphous pigment. Skin is a remarkable organ that can manufacture vitamin D from sunlight alone. It excretes toxins. Just under the epidermis are thousands of sensory nerve endings for tactile sensitivity. The hands, in particular, are just full of them. Stab a thorn into the bare flesh of your palm, and you'll notice right away; run a tiller for an hour without gloves, and it will take a little longer to assess the nerve damage. Even the blessings of civilization are hard on human hands.

Look at your hands: fingers that curl, perfect for adorning with golden rings, palms crisscrossed with lines of fate, love, and longevity, maybe an honest callus or two, with an opposable thumb on each front paw that is the envy of cats and dogs everywhere. The hand is a tool of unsurpassed dexterity, the main tool of a tool-making species.

Hands can pick up a coconut or a snowflake, count tiny seeds or lift watermelons, stroke a lover or field-strip an automatic weapon. The dominant hand can write poems, almost by itself, or paint a picture; after a hard day of one-handed creation, the other can apply soothing lotion to the back of the artsy hand. We interpret the world through our hands; they ratify the evidence of our other senses. Hands come in all colors and two versions, left and right.

Now take these tools and dig in the dirt with them. Don't be afraid; you have two hands, so one of them must be a spare. Plunge them into the pathogenic soil, filled with worms, spiders, snakes, and gophers.

At a cocktail party in Colorado many years back, a man told me about the time he was working in his garden, and he punched through into a gopher tunnel at the precise moment when the gopher was passing through. This animal had been predating his garden for weeks. Thinking quickly, he seized it in his bare hands.

Now on his thumb he had a scar, E-I-E-I-O. He admitted that grabbing a live bull gopher was probably a mistake. He wasn't wearing gloves, partly because of his profession; he was a cultural anthropologist and had lived with primitive tribes in South America. In those villages, he said, gloves would have been considered high technology. The men wore sheathes made of bark or hide, the women wore strings made of woven grass or hair, and the children went naked except for mud until puberty. Everyone constantly touched the dirt with their hands; that day, working in his garden, he was trying to bridge a cultural gap, exploring the sense of being really, really dirty as a way of life, when he came upon the gopher.

Over several drinks, he explained further: "In some cultures, that would be like finding the day's protein for a whole family. When you're handed a gift by the spirits in that way, what do you do? You grab it, before it gets away."

With a pure and natural malice, the gopher bit through the meat of his thumb and locked its jaw; fortunately, the flesh ripped when the hand was shaken vigorously, and the gopher broke off the attack. There was real blood coursing down his arm. "I flashed, man," he said. "At that moment, I could feel five thousand years of civilization sloughing off."

And so when I think about the two options available, to wear gloves or not, the heuristic imprint in my mind is of that knotted scar on his thumb. It looked as if someone had driven a car key under the thumbprint, given it a twist, and then lifted. He also detailed the way he had revenged himself on the gopher, which we'll come to presently.

At the start of each year, my hands go inside a new pair of leather gloves, brown, size XL, with a heavenly smell, and made in the gunn pattern. May your Scrabble skills increase to know that there are two methods of cutting and sewing gloves: gunn and clute. Utterly useless information, compared to the sensory feedback from your hands when you slip them inside. My old gloves are scarred, weathered, and ripped from a year's use. They smell of manure and sweat; they are grimy with nose oil and slug slime, earth and ashes. Without gloves, my hands would have endured direct contact with those things.

Sometimes I wear out two pairs of leather gloves per season, always the right one first. Joy makes one pair last for five years. I wear gloves religiously, no matter what tool I'm using. For the most part, Joy rarely wears gloves. It's a personal decision.

Gloves

There are two schools of thought on wearing gloves. I will begin with some pro-glove arguments. First of all, dirt is dirty. I learned this at the age of three, making mudpies for personal consumption. Since it had been freshly decanted from the cat bowl, the water alone could not have imparted the awful taste and grittiness. The other ingredient was dirt, and I have never trusted it since. I don't particularly like it adhering to my hands or drying under my fingernails, either. Grandmothers may tell children that everyone has to eat a peck of dirt over the course of their lives, and it may be true, but no one says it has to make contact with our hands.

Now try this. Wash your hands in water heated to 110 degrees Fahrenheit, with some lavender soap and a good nail brush. Dry them on a thick towel and rub a little vegetable oil into them. Slip your hands into some really fine gardening gloves, flexible as your own skin but a lot tougher, with that rich leather smell. If you cannot smell the aforementioned, you are in the majority: gloved gardeners who favor cloth. Now work in the garden for several hours.

Gloves for gardeners should be light and cool in the summer, warm and comforting in the winter. If you wear gloves, this means you'll need two pairs, one of them insulated with fleece. Try on several types in the store, if possible, or order them from a reliable garden catalog. Even canvas gloves, especially the kind with multiple rubber dots on the palm, will protect your hands from sunburn, blisters, and puncture wounds, although for weeding, leather is definitely superior.

If you favor leather, your options include skins from sheep, goats, pigs, cows, and deer. Goatskin wears the best, even though it's soft; goatskin gloves may be hard to find, but they're worth the search. Cowhide is good, especially for weeding thorns and thistles. Next in order of preference would be deerskin or elkhide; those gloves are expensive and soft, but they wear out quickly. Pigskin gloves don't last more than half a season in our garden, so I've stopped using them.

There are things to be said for a natural approach, so let's say them. Our friend, Prudence, has no use for gloves. She holds up her hands: "These are my best garden tools. I've gotta feel what I'm doing. Wearing gloves in a garden is like making love with a condom." Prudence is an earth person and an expert gardener. When the devas call to her, she claims, she must immerse herself in the dirt, reaching down to her elbows to connect with the soil. "I like to get really, really dirty when I work in the garden. Sweaty is even better."

TOOLS OF THE EARTH

After lengthy interviews with local gardeners, I diffidently offer what seems to be a pattern: Many more women than men seem to prefer to garden without gloves. Moreover, many women have recently stopped wearing gloves; if they've read certain books, you won't find a glove in the house. Obviously, wearing gloves cannot be a gender-specific preference, but let's examine some putative reasons for not wearing them. Perhaps men go gloveless, in part, to get in touch with their basic manliness, the rough beast that roams the savannah. Possibly, more women are going gloveless to get in touch with the earth, to unite with its subtle magic. Now let's tiptoe out of this PC minefield and walk out to the garden.

Remove your gloves and plunge your hands into the cool brown soil. Take it a step further: remove all your clothes, put on sunblock, and spend an hour or so weeding in the buff, just as an experiment. At first you will quiver with modesty, even if no one is watching but birds. But soon you get into the fun of it: the warm sun on your back, the breeze blowing where it customarily bloweth not, and a serene, savage sense of being at one with Nature. At the end of that time, if no one catches you, your gardening experience will seem as exotic and exciting as a trip to Paris. Feeling the sun beat on your naked flanks, pushing earth up between every toe, you will understand your own garden as never before.

Another argument for nude gardening: Counting the price of hat, boots, shirt, pants, kneepads, and gloves, we arrive at a cost between ten and two hundred dollars. The cheapest, most natural way to garden is naked. Personally, I'm happy to spend the money, believing that it is dangerous to succumb to primitive racial memories. Naked once or twice is fine, but it is too easy to go native.

For cheap gloves, go to a pharmacy and obtain a box of six latex dermatological gloves, the kind surgeons wear, if not of the same quality. They are very reasonably priced. These gloves allow a tactile sensitivity that some gardeners find comfortable, perhaps even exciting. The savings is offset by the fact that latex will only keep your hands clean, not protect them from gophers, blackberry vines, or the bite of an assassin bug. Squish its body and its jaws stay clamped, and it must be removed with needle-nosed pliers. Latex gloves are not a prophylactic for snakebite, either, nor cuts from a razor-sharp hoe knife. Most damning of all, they're disposable.

My advice: always put these two fine garden tools inside supple leather gloves, where splinter cannot stab, thorn prick, nor slug beslime. Rub a little ointment on the gloves before you don them—either Vaseline, Bag Balm, or just peanut oil—and your hands will be fresh and happy after a hard day in the garden. They will be civilized hands.

The man in Colorado told me the rest of the story, and I've debated about passing it along. After all, he was a man who liked to work with his hands, to garden in the rough, to make that savage connection with his earliest ancestors by getting his paws filthy, and his reasons were commendable. You might think that, after the bandages came off, he bought a pair of stout leather work gloves made of split rhinoceros hide, with gauntlet extensions reaching to his armpits, thereby bolstering my point about gloves. We have developed civilization to cope with these things.

But no. His academic interest was whetted, and he felt close to the primitive, natural response, unfettered by concepts of morality. He had uncovered one of the raw dangers of gardening, paying for this knowledge with his lifeblood. Like Rima in Hudson's classic *Green Mansions*, which he had read, he came into perfect harmony with himself. The wind and the sky told him what to do next.

He sharpened a shovel handle into a crude spear and hardened the point with fire, using his gas grill. He began stalking the gopher, mapping its tunnel complex, watching its routine for lapses in security. One day, he found and killed it. Then he—well.

We had both been drinking quite a bit. Sometimes, around a campfire or a cocktail, a guy will spill his most secret story, the one not even his wife or colleagues will ever hear. He told me the rest of it, which will not be set forth here. The image might haunt you every time you saw a gopher volcano. In many ways, though, it was the most interesting part. At all events, he could return to his adopted people with the badge, and scars, of a warrior.

One touch of nature makes the whole world kin.

♦

SHAKESPEARE

AUGER

The Science of Holes

Someone has been digging in the compost pile, and all the evidence points to a certain bad dog. I could fence him out of the yard, perhaps, but our little freehold is enclosed enough, with a gate to keep cars out of the yard and the pasture fenced off to keep the horse out of the garden. Joy seems to think we don't need a fence around the garden proper; something there is that does not love a wall, and it's called a Vermonter. But she may change her mind this year when deer and raccoons come by to sample the corn.

However, I see her point about too many fences. There's only a shade of difference between enclosure and confinement. Test the bars of your own cage sometime. Fencing dogs out means fencing us in.

A removable gate in front would keep animals out and still let us in to fork it. If I dig four holes and drop in four posts, and wrap all but the south side in garden wire, that's a good start. I can start filling it up with compost immediately and make the gate later. The more I think about this, the more attractive the idea gets. Half a day of hard work should do it.

"Don't forget to put a divider down the middle," Joy advises when I'm drawing it out on the kitchen table after supper. "So we can turn the pile and put the bottom stuff on the top." Okay, that means a double-sized compost bin and two additional posts. Growing up in rocky New England, Joy learned a lot about composting. I have the basic theory of piles down, but it seems like a lot of work when compared to the new composting tumblers. Someday I might make one out of a plastic barrel, locally available from a soft-drink bottling plant, just to see how one works.

Late the next morning, I round up the posts; not treated posts, which are soaked in poison, but six good peeled locust poles that will last fifty years. According to the calendar, the new moon is less than a week away, so even that mystical base is covered. You're supposed to put fence posts in when the moon is waning, if you

believe in that stuff; otherwise the post will be loose because the wood swells in harmony with the moon. That's what they say, anyway.

The proper technique for drilling a posthole by hand is something that is better watched than described, but the basics are easy to grasp: you want a deep, plumb hole. With this firmly in mind, take the clamshell diggers in both hands, to get the feel of it, and then lift, drop, and spread the handles until the hole goes down about six inches. Turn the tool ninety degrees, lift, and drop again.

Don't get in the habit of driving the clamshells into the earth with mighty blows because you'll already be sore enough when the auger gets through with your hands, forearms, and splenius. I take fifteen minutes to dig a posthole, stopping every now and then to commune with hummingbirds and stretch my back. Even then, my entire neck assembly, shoulders, sacrum, and pelvic girdle will feel like they need an ambulance at day's end. But it's a good kind of tired, the fatigue of honest work.

Dig down about a foot with the clamshells. The earth is soft and black, just moist enough to bore easily. That was nice, wasn't it? At one foot deep, you've got a good start for the next tool, which is an auger. Drop the auger head in the fresh hole, and we all hope your auger is not too big to fit. Some augers are adjustable, with blades that can be widened or narrowed by moving two bolts. Some aren't. There isn't a lot of variation in the hand-operated posthole auger design.

Turn the auger one-quarter of a circle at a time, and don't try for a full 180-degree twist, which strains back muscles into chiropractor country; heed the voice of experience. Four turns should equal one full revolution. Pull the auger out frequently as it fills up with loose dirt, and save this in a wheelbarrow to add to the compost.

Rental shops carry a power auger that two persons can operate, after which, I suspect, their spinal columns must be replaced. I've used one before, and it was considerably faster. Some tractors can be fitted with a hydraulic-lift auger; that's the easiest, most expensive, least simple, most resource-gobbling way to dig postholes, using fossil fuels to make a hole in the earth. But if you must bore, say, five hundred holes to fence off a big pasture, you will have no choice.

Alternatively, you can buy three tools: the clamshell, auger, and rock bar. These are sufficient for the few holes most people need to dig, and you can pass these tools down to your descendants. This purchase will cost between ten and seventy-five dollars, depending on your buying habits: about ten cents a hole over the average lifetime.

Personally, I've limited my greed for fencepost tools to a new clamshell and auger with fiberglass shafts. They're a bit heavier than my old tools, but virtually unbreakable. I had to replace the handles on the old clamshells five years ago, and they look like they've got another five left.

Many winters ago, I met an old cowboy named Casey in a bus station on a snowy day in Wyoming. He rolled his own smokes and spoke at a slow, easy trot. On the bus, we got talking about life, his life in particular, and he told me that he had made 9,784 holes with clamshells and augers, by hand, up in Montana. Casey had worked as a cowhand on a cattle ranch called the Meanwhile, up in the Bighorns; he was good with numbers, although he couldn't read. He told me how he got the job in 1949, and recounted most of the subsequent events until he dug his last hole in 1955.

Out on the range, he'd also seen a few flying saucers, skimming along in formation above the lonely grasslands; he said this in a matter-of-fact Western drawl. Back at the Meanwhile ranch, he had been generally disbelieved, "until we started finding mule-ated cows. Tongues gone, butts cored out, guts missin'. Fella come out from the state and said it was coyotes." He snorted. "But the vet told him he never saw a coyote use a scalpel that good."

In those years, his legs had become bowed from riding horses all day long. His knuckles were scarred, no doubt from punching cows. His back had curved forward and fused, so he largely resembled a wishbone; he couldn't bring his head any higher than his shoulders. I was going to silently resolve never to touch a posthole tool again, but in the course of the monologue, Casey explained that he had been kicked in the back by a horse, right between his shoulder blades. After he got out of the hospital, he dug no more holes. "Don't never turn your back on a horse," was Casey's final word on that subject.

Behind me, Ren's mare crops grass with a chomping sound while I set the posts and backfill them with gravel. After the hole is augered to a sufficient depth, I drop the post in a few times to tamp the base and kill the microscopic bugs that cause rot. Then I pour in a shovelful of large gravel and drop the post a few more times. This might make the soil microbes so punchy that they won't begin attacking these

untreated posts for days. Next job: fill around the posts with gravel, shaking them all the while to help the tiny rocks settle in. Finally, I paint the top of each post with tar, and they should outlast the fence wire.

Done. My new auger and clamshell are superior to my old ones with the wooden handles in every way; the digging went faster, the blisters are much more clearly defined and larger, and the time required to return my back to normalcy has increased by 50 percent, owing to the extra weight. But on the plus side of the ledger, the fiberglass handles make the clamshells work a little better. It's only the side effects that hurt.

Time to stretch the fence wire around those three posts, using new staples and the last of my recycled ones. It's good policy to recover staples from old fence posts, to keep them from winding up in tires or horse hooves. These are fascinating fasteners. Take a close look at the cut points on each leg of a U-shaped fence staple, and note how they're cut on the bias and reversed; that's so the legs of the staple will spread apart in different directions when driven, to hold better. Obviously, some thought went into their design.

I hose off the digging tools and set them in the sun to dry while I round up a hammer, some fence pliers, the can of staples, and a pair of safety glasses. You might not fancy the concept of wearing eye protection for para-gardening work like putting in fences. But wire can whip back suddenly, going right for your face, and then it's out-vile-jelly for one or both of your optics. I managed to scratch a cornea recently when a fir branch snapped back and caught me full in the eyeball. A scratched cornea feels exactly like a hairy tennis ball wedged under an eyelid. I didn't think I needed eye protection for a simple job like pruning trees.

When the job is done, I step back and admire it. Our compost heap will be easier to turn, much more tidy, and literally squared away. A job well done. My body feels tired down to its tiniest bones, but that's offset, as always, by the warm glow of accomplishment.

If you want knowledge, you must toil for it.

◆

RUSKIN

HAMMOCK

Alone at last. Joy has gone to Mootown for the day, Ren is away all week at camp, and I have been laboring in the garden, murdering bugs and ripping out weeds and shoveling manure under a blazing sun. It's as muggy as a steam bath.

Of all the tools of the earth, of all the things we use to till, seed, shape, water, harrow, rake, weed, and harvest our happy gardens, the hammock is the only one that will make us feel better immediately. Of all the raised beds in the garden, only the hammock cures fatigue.

To begin treating fatigue before the onset of serious symptoms, let every muscle sag as you lay back on the hammock; now, very slowly, flip your legs up, finding the balance, seeking suspension. Proper mounting is critical. Never fall back on a hammock. Straddle it if you must, but always be careful when lying down. This is the moment when hammock novices fall out, especially in a narrow hammock. The wider the hammock, the more stable it is.

Ours, fortunately, is a long, two-person hammock, of the size called a *matrimonial*, or "marriage bed," in Mexico. A minute of gentle rocking before the hammock and the body attain equilibrium, and then sweet, sweet rest.

There is a profoundly spiritual dimension to gardening, and I suspect it has something to do with hard work in the service of the earth. Perhaps the truly enlightening moments come while running a garden tool, such as a hoe. The story is told of a monk sweeping stairs, whose broom flips a pebble into a wall, *pok!* He stops sweeping; in that echoing moment, he understands the nature of Zen, his place in the universe, and what all those koans are about.

For many hours I have uprooted weeds, waiting for some secret realization. Part of Zen is the patience to wait and do the work. Chop sod, haul water.

The other part is called "just sitting." That's what I try to do when resting in a

hammock, but from the supine position. Breath goes in, breath goes out. Sometimes, sleep follows.

It's a wonderful life, but you don't have to be conscious for all of it. When you're confused by too many data downloads, sleep is the best medicine. When consciousness prods you too hard, sleep heals all the simultaneous and incompatible emotions. Nothing beats that state of sleep where you can actually hear yourself snore while you're still conscious. At that hovering stage of the mind-shutdown process, you can almost see the Great Oz pulling levers behind the curtain. Your dreams can come true, quite literally.

This book, for instance, began as a daydream in this hammock. Quite a lot of it was written in here, between spurts of hard work with the selfsame hardware pictured between its covers.

There is a straight-line connection between hard work and success. But dreams must come first, and that requires time to review the goal in mind, to see if it's a worthy investment of your life. Sometimes resting and wandering can speed the journey. Let me tell you about my old friend, Jack.

Last summer I was in downtown Eugene, a city so cosmopolitan and yet so earthy that it is sometimes called "Venice of the Northwest" or "Berkeley, Oregon." There I found a large but comfortable store called Down to Earth, entirely dedicated to gardening. I bought a few tools and some supplies, and then asked the clerk if, by chance, she had ever heard of Jack. It seemed logical and possible; he was the best gardener I'd ever met, and Eugene was the last place I'd seen him, in 1973.

The woman behind the register blinked. "Yes . . . he's president of this company."

It was my turn to blink. The last time I'd seen Jack, he was living out of a backpack and eating road food. One dark night Before Watergate, we each picked six green apples from a tree and said farewell, not knowing where either of us would wind up: two long-haired individuals of good will and small means, traveling our separate roads together. At the time, those dozen apples were about the extent of our combined wealth.

I took my six Granny Smiths and, twenty years later, had parlayed it into a career as a self-unemployed freelance writer. But Jack had done better; he was now the CEO of an earth-friendly corporation, dedicated to gardening globally in a gentle and benign way.

His commitment to that goal began early. Once, he had walked away from a good job with the state forestry department because they told him to spray alder saplings with herbicide. He refused. "Do it or hit the road," they told him. He hit the road. Illogical as it may seem, quitting that job was a step toward finding his life's work and future success.

Oddly enough, he remembered me, and even recalled that fateful night. We had both grown older, gotten haircuts, started families, and kept our ideals polished. These days, Jack spends a lot of time fishing from a boat, which is essentially hours of unbroken thought, just like gardening. His business prospers, and even has a nice Web site.

I hung this hammock about five years ago. Uphill from our garden, under an old locust tree, I paced out twelve feet toward the garden and sank a treated post securely in the ground to hold the other end of a cotton hammock from L.L. Bean. It's not in full shade; a little dappled sunlight leaks in between the locust leaves. On the other side of the tree hangs a punching bag. It's a very therapeutic place when one is either fatigued or frustrated.

It's hard to say when the hammock became so popular, moving in on the Adirondack chair and the time-honored wooden glider in the garden resting spot. The rope *hamaca* probably traveled to the United States from Mexico, where it's a common outdoor bed, but the name came from the West Indies. It's an old design for sleeping furniture.

Some might question my case for the hammock as a garden tool. Stipulated: The mind is a tool. The human body is also a tool, and this tool needs maintenance in the form of respite from hard work. Just as a file is a tool for honing a hoe, the hammock is a tool for easing the edge of a dull mind. Thoughts wander. Worries vanish. Aches subside. The people rest.

And so do I, when the sun is too hot to keep weeding, when the air begins to swim with little spots in front of my eyes. When the garden is too much with me, I lie down. Resting outside can't be done in the long indoor months of winter, so that leaves the summer, four or five months tops. The garden will not grow faster than I can keep up, so there's no rush. As Will Durant wrote, "No one who is in a hurry is quite civilized."

Not that the hammock is chiropractically correct, but it's situated in the path of cool breezes, under a spreading locust in bloom, a hundred feet of thorny branches and mint-green foliage. I never see it without thinking about fence posts. Small locust trees make the best posts. During the Depression, local farmers paid their county taxes with timber, including fence posts from fifteen-year-old locusts.

This tree is exactly like life: thorny, rough, grows quickly, pretty at times and ugly at others, useful, no one is forcing us to climb to the top; and underneath its sheltering boughs, there is a bed to make it all disappear, and a whole universe to explore on this side of our eyelids.

The hammock has begun to rock and roll. Dogananda invariably waits until the hammock is occupied to walk under it, back and forth, scratching his back with dreamy eyes and incidentally giving me a bumpy massage, a sort of canine Magic Fingers. Dog was born here, and he sports the black-and-tan paint job of a Rottweiler but otherwise has the body and soul of a black Labrador. He seldom makes a sound. His mother, Ma, was a spaniel mix who did most of the barking necessary to the maintenance of a well-guarded farm. She's gone now, buried in the shade under an apple tree.

Oxtayle Acre is not really a farm, of course. It is one single acre in the country, adjacent to square miles of uninhabited tree farm. The only other house nearby is far to the west, belonging to my brother and his family. We have limited livestock: one cat, two dogs, one horse, one white dove, and twenty chickens. Apart from the chickens, all the resident fauna are companion animals for our daughter.

When he's done scratching, Dog goes away to inspect a gopher hole, and I go back to my ruminations. There is a monumental amount to learn about gardening and about life. Killing our television was a good step toward finding more time for living. One way to tackle vast amounts of information is to ignore it, to purposely turn away and let news leak into us, if it must, by osmosis. While this occurs, we can read and loaf.

Already today I have learned a new word: *symphylan*. For gardeners, it means "enemy." While looking it up in the dictionary, I learned also that "sunt" is the wood of the bablah tree. Thus my knowledge of arboriculture expands, even by kicking back.

I am about to fade to black when a friend phones. Muck, short for Malachi, has caught me asleep with a dictionary on my chest and a cordless phone nearby. "Snoring away the afternoon" is all he says, almost wistfully. "I gotta get me a hammock." Muck's a gardener when he can find the time, so I ask him about symphylans.

"That's sim-fillans," he says, "or symphilids, like the social disease. You got 'em?"

I explain that I don't know even what they are, aside from a nearly microscopic suborder of insects, practically invisible, and (of course) unfriendly to gardens. But if our garden was infested, what do symphylans do? For that matter, what are they?

Muck defines them with a string of obscenities. Right away, I gather that *Scutigerella immaculata* is the dirtiest Latin name he knows. "You better hope you don't have them. They live in horseshit and they kill brassicas. Ten of them would fit on your thumbnail. They're fast as silverfish, and they eat the root tips even before plants sprout," he says, strangling the phone. "One year, your beets and cauliflower and spinach come right up, but next year, it's like you didn't even plant. They abort everything." He discusses what he'd like to do to them, slowly and with tweezers, and what can be done practically: diatomaceous earth, the silicated shells of ancient sealife, can be spread everywhere. It cuts them up like microscopic razors and stabs them between the armor plates of their exoskeletons and carapaces, which croaks them by exsanguination.

"Which is good, I hope they die screaming for someone to pull it out, but that stuff's really expensive, especially if you have to scatter it all over your garden. Not good for your lungs, either. And on a humid day, insects don't bleed fast enough to die. No, the only thing that even thins out symphylans is Dyfonate." Muck rates that stuff close to plutonium on the toxicity scale. It's highly restricted because a tiny amount can kill you dead.

These bugs are imported from Europe or Asia, I'll bet everything down to my last dime. All the really vicious pests come from overseas, I say.

"*Pas du tout,*" Muck replies. "They were here all along, probably in symbiotic balance for thousands of years with the old-growth forest floor. Hey. You see any ancient cathedral forests out by your place? Any towering redwoods, any forest primevals?"

I check. Nope, no more old-growth forest, just shaved hilltops going fuzzy with young Doug Fir, a few scuzzy patches of as yet uncut third-growth timber, and our garden. I grew up here, and the forest has changed immensely since then. Muck snorts. "In a healthy ecology, everything's connected to everything else, right? I think clear-cutting sent the symphylans onto cultivated land," Muck concludes.

He blames everything that is wrong with Oregon, including the weather, on the timber harvests over the last 150 years. He backs it up with a lot of hard evidence, and he often recites: "You don't 'harvest' a thousand-year-old forest if you didn't plant it." Predictably, he says it again now. We yak a bit longer about the perfidies of symphylans and the corporate timber industry, and hang up.

I fire up the laptop to run a quick search on the Net for more information, and type a few notes in my garden journal:

"Memo: Get some diatomaceous earth, just in case. Whether or not we have symphylans, it also kills thrips, mites, earwigs, slugs, cornworms, hornworms, flies, aphids, and spider mites. Note: It also kills beneficial insects. Addendum: hold off on d. earth for a while. Establish if symphs. present in grdn. Ask neighbors. Ask Joy."

Instead of sleeping, I decide to write, letting the thoughts float for a minute. Before words ever go down on pixels or paper, writing is a state of intense focus; before that, however, writing is pure perception, like taking a kayak down into the chaotic maelstrom of consciousness, from which a central concept may emerge. Or it may not, and then you stare at the blank screen of your own consciousness for long moments. With practice, you can compose entire pages in a mental notebook, and keep them long enough to get to a keyboard. It's not an easy trick. The hammock is a perfect place to practice.

By the time Joy gets home, I'm back in the garden, refreshed and weeding.

It was such a lovely day, I thought it a pity to get up.

◆

SOMERSET MAUGHAM

GRUB HOE

Ground Zero

It's a windy day in the middle of the growing season as I write in the garden journal, typing at full speed:

"One weed left to pull, down by the edge of the garden. After a search on the Internet for ways to get it out, I found that I was using the right tool all along. For one great big weed or a mat of closely packed and firmly rooted weeds, a sturdy grub hoe is" [here, the screen goes dark]—the lights flicker, the computer comes back on, all heretofore utterly deleted. We give thanks for the blessings of technology, from dependable hot water to cantankerous computers. Start over:

"The grub hoe is more reliable than the computer, if not nearly as versatile. When I'm" [the power dies again, this time for whole seconds]—the house seems to pass out and then wake up again, humming.

Try once more: "All right, the computer as a garden tool has blown its last chance to have its own chapter. Instead, the lowly grub hoe will be elevated, because it always works, doesn't rely on high technology to operate. Given the choice between a life of using the grub hoe, which functions in all weather and has been field-tested for the last fifty thousand years, and running the computer, a relatively new gizmo which is prone to failure, pick the grub hoe. Although the computer can be useful to gardeners who are willing to wrestle and pin it, the first time an hour's work is" [the screen blacks out again]—erased from existence without possibility of appeal.

Sometimes computers catch viruses, as this one did a few months ago, sucking billions of bytes down into darkness, including a rather complimentary essay on itself. The hard drive has been scraped clean, virus-protected, and backed up seven ways, but the machine itself is undependable.

At least the phone works. "Hi. Sure, I'll hold. Hi, I'd like to report some brownouts and voltage spikes out here, and I wonder if there's any danger of the power going out. Whatsun. You don't—thank you, of course Dispatch would know. Hi, we've

had some brownouts here—Whatsun—and I wonder if the power is going to stay on. I'm on a deadline."

Dispatch laughs. He says they have only one circuit open in this vicinity, and that it's a miracle that I still have any juice because the wind's knocked out most of the grid. If I'm working on a computer, he says, best to save everything and get off. So I do, typing and mousing frantically, stuffing data onto a disk, but it does not exactly get me off.

When it works, this tool is a marvel. On the hard drive of the computer is an existential garden, with vast encyclopedias of plants and bugs, a garden journal already set in type with scanned pictures, and not one speck of dirt anywhere. With the aid of software, it grows flowers that no hand will ever pick, fruits that no tongue will ever taste; it exists only as north-south domains of binary information in a magnetic universe. Theoretically, our virtual garden mirrors the real one. Both were carefully considered before we ever broke ground with sweat and a grub hoe.

This was an experiment, the first attempt to plan our garden on a computer. In this reality, the corn patch flourishes, the flowers bloom, and the pH is perfect; water magically appears in the ground; pixeled marigolds repel flea beetles, and iconic nasturtiums repel aphids. The whole cyber-garden ticks like a clock.

But it isn't reality. Back in the meatspace, a weird virus is attacking one tomato plant, and the computer database offers no cure except death. The corn patch has been decimated by various wildlife, and the marigolds are wilting from water deprivation. The damnable nasturtiums are actually attracting aphids, but I haven't had time to update the nasturtium as a catch plant. The real garden smells of neglect and disorder.

Nevertheless, we keep track of what's happening. A typical entry on disk: "Hot day all week. Raccoon bandits none, but squirrel gang taking over. Found a cornstalk halfway up an alder tree in east wildwood. Entry/exit made at gap in electric fence; plug tomorrow. Set out Claymores? Weeds have pretty good beachhead in southern bed. Eggplant needs more water. Fix hose. Bone meal on potatoes, or not? Check w/Joy. Visit Garden Chat, ask Darth Vetch, Callalilly, or Crocuspocus about squirrel control. Lion poop to ward off?" Notes like these keep us on top of the garden, but we need big dams to read them, or nuclear power stations.

Five minutes later, the power crashes for good. Our electronic garden journal is down for the day, but the paper backup is due for an update. For years, we've kept our hard-copy garden journal in a three-ring binder with a worn leather cover. Affirmations are scrawled all over the cover in ink: LEARN TO WELCOME AD-VERSITY FOR ITS LESSONS. HOE, HOE, HOE. IT DOESN'T RAIN EVERY DAY. LOOK FOR DEVAS. PLANT A ROW FOR THE HUNGRY. BILLION-AIRES JUST HAVE DIFFERENT PROBLEMS. SOW LOVE, HARVEST PEACE. THE FAMILY THAT GARDENS TOGETHER PARDONS THE WEATHER. THE GREEN MAN WAS HERE. And so forth.

These are more positive than a few of the collected epigrams on the hard-drive jour-nal, such as the quote from historian William Bolitho: "The whole of Nature hope-fully awaits the day we shall be extinct." That one seemed a bit over the top, but it fit in the Doomsday file, where I'm researching types of vegetables that could be grown during a nuclear winter. In the terrain of cyberspace, there are limitless possibilities, and all questions have answers.

As a gardener's tool, a journal ranks at the exact midpoint between a computer and a grub hoe on the scale of utility. It requires attention, preferably daily entries but at least regular notes, to create a current record. Next year, for instance, we can com-pare the previous year's weather, corn height, composting conditions, and any weed and bug problems extant on July 12. Theoretically, a computer makes this record-keeping easier.

Feel free to experiment in a garden journal; there's no right or wrong way to keep one, and not having one at all is fine, too. Some gardeners go so far as to color in plotted diagrams, make graph charts, and duly log the weight of each harvest in grams. Others ignore the statistics and fill their journals with fanciful descriptions of flower beds singing in chorus, or the way hummingbirds joust.

For half an hour, sitting by a window for light, I write a longhand progress report on the garden, covering the topic that my computer spaced: A week-long struggle to remove a big weed in the real world. Taking the definition of a weed as any plant growing where you don't want it to, a young alder tree qual-ified because it was shading the corn.

First, I chopped it into firewood with a chainsaw, ignoring the pollutants being coughed into the atmosphere. Only the root remains. I left the stump high, a handle

to help extract it. There are lots of ways to get rid of stumps, depending on your schedule. You can cut a stump flush, drill holes in the top, fill it with fertilizer, and wait for it to rot. This is very natural, but it can take years. A tractor would pull it in five minutes with the aid of a chain and lever bar, and probably burn less than a gallon of diesel. I've blown stumps before, which is great fun; dynamite would shatter this stump in one second, as well as all our kitchen windows. Joy has already vetoed this idea. Explosives might add valuable nitrates to the soil, she said, but the devas would get nosebleeds and fly away forever.

A grub hoe can accomplish the job in a few days, the old-fashioned way. It's not easy work, but no computer on earth could do it. And with a grub hoe, there is no danger that ground you have already broken up will seal itself behind you into a compact mat.

It's also a good tool for severe weed conditions. As each bed is harvested, I run the tiller through the soil and then plumb forget about it. You know how it is: a week slips by, and then two, and suddenly weeds have marched in and taken over a fallow garden bed.

A weed in loose soil gives up when it sees an ordinary hoe coming, but a carpet of grass and nongrass weeds is seamless, so I have to use a grub hoe, grape hoe, or mattock. There are slight differences in blade width and design, but they are all in the same adze family, and they all remove tough weeds and break up compacted dirt. After skimming it with a shovel, peeling up the matted sod and setting it aside (and upside-down), I begin smiting the earth with the grub hoe. It's probably the same way the first agriculturalists did it, whacking the soil with a crude paddle. Each swing chops out another clump of weeds and sod, breaking up the dirt eight inches deep. When it's loose enough, I make a few passes with the tiller and call it a day.

Afterward, there is no pleasure on earth that exceeds the delight of a hot bath. But if you want to try, stack on more sensual delights: a warm starry evening, a good cigar, fine brandy in a mug of hot chocolate, two big Turkish towels, and a white bathrobe made of spun sheep souls. All these are the gifts of an abundant civilization.

Being clean is a luxury, like computers and soap. In primitive societies, hot water does not come out of a tap. It must be handmade. Hot water is the first basic luxury, the one that must have astounded the earliest human in need of a bath. A basket of water got too close to the fire, a dirty hand pulled it away, and the bugs and grime peeled right off. After rubbing with a few campfire ashes, so did those clumps of mammoth fat stuck under the fingernails for the last six weeks. In the search for new creature comforts, civilization began.

It will be interesting to see how it ends. Not long ago, I typed in a computer search for "millennial prophecy," just for a dose of cheap terror. The dates for doom range from 1914 to 2012, but they tend to congregate around the turn of the millennium. That night, I had a dream in which I saw civilization as a giant pyramid, not made of stone blocks but fantastically intricate and continually under construction, with billions of moving parts, and occupied by intellectually gifted mammals. In its own complicated way, civilization was quite beautiful. Oddly enough, it was an attempt to reach the perfection of the divine, a recurring experiment throughout history. To build this magnificent edifice was a tropism as natural to humans as a tree growing toward the sun.

However, it was upside-down. This pyramid had been constructed with its apex resting on the earth. Even so, its stability was perfect, at least so far; such was the technical perfection of its builders that, for all its mass, it rose skyward in nearly absolute equilibrium. The base continued to spread outward and upward, and it revolved slowly enough to give it a nice gyroscopic effect that further improved its balance.

Not all was well. Millions of people were crawling up all four sides, trying to get to the top where all the real wealth was kept. They kept being flung off by the spin, their deaths mostly unremarked. And I saw further in my vision, with a horrifying clarity: a single fly was circling, picking a corner to land upon. When that happened, the inevitable laws of physics would take over. I bolted up from the dream, input a cup of coffee and a few cigarettes, and then headed out to the garden with a grub hoe.

Years back, we were having supper at the home of an acquaintance and his wife when the subject of nuclear war came up. Dr. Mattock was not his name, but his comments indicated that he thought the grub hoe was coming back in a big way. He had opinions, and they were educated opinions—possible scenarios, political outcomes, and duration of nuclear conflict. "Hours, probably," he said,

"or maybe days if the Asian nations get into it. But by no means more than a week." He assessed the degree of likelihood that a nuclear weapon would someday reduce a city to slag: "Within the next twenty-five years, almost a certainty." He spoke of nuclear exchange as if it were some kind of horrible, inevitable barter.

This supper happened less than twenty-five years ago. Computers were not common then, but now we know that the first electromagnetic pulse would take them all down forever. Instant hot water would be the next casualty. Famine would follow, and growing our own food would no longer be a choice. This is all just projection, a misuse of the imagination, but sometimes it can seem very real.

This summer, we spent a Saturday afternoon atop the highest peak in the coast range, with a panoramic view of the Willamette Valley. Below, dozens of giant mushroom clouds rose up, their smokey dark heads roiling furiously. This is an annual event, as grass-seed farmers burn their fields to sterilize the earth, killing weeds and enriching the soil with potash at the same time. The perimeter is fired, creating a chimney effect that pulls the smoke straight up.

Not everyone is delighted about this spectacle, but the grass-seed farmers have a powerful lobby, and they point to the fact that the Indians burned the grass off in the Valley long before the first settlers arrived. For years, environmentalists have fought the burning with lawsuits and protests. Still, it's a beautiful sort of cautionary performance art, a sky-painted gallery: "Thermonuclear Blossoms over Cultivated Land." I took a picture and pasted it in the garden journal, over a bit of Wendell Berry's wisdom: "The more technological sophistication we have attained, the more destructive we have become . . ."

Earth abides, so far. If the planet's still here tomorrow, and it surely will be, I'll be out in the garden, swinging a grub hoe. That stump is doomed.

Prediction is very hard, especially when it's about the future.

◆

YOGI BERRA

LOPPERS

Clear-cut Issues

The sign on the tree surgeon's truck said "Expert Pruning" in big cartoon letters. I was working on a hillside construction site in the middle of a forest that overlooked a teeming industrial supercity, although fir branches hid most of it. To the carpenters, a natural view was preferable to any vista of smokestacks and urban sprawl, but the owner brought in a specialist to "prune the trees and let in some daylight." Without any apparent plan, the young tree doctor put on his climbing spurs and began lopping off all the low branches around the trunk, climbing as he cut. He left a minuscule Christmas tree at the top, a pitiful photosynthetic knob.

"Of all the incompetent . . . he *poodled* that damn tree," one carpenter said. "It'll die now." After a few more trees got their medicine, the city stood revealed, seen through the naked trees like a glistening, swarming ant farm. Over a week's time, all the rest of the downhill trees received the same pruning protocol; a few years later, every one succumbed and had to be cut. We carpenters thought it was a damn crime, and accused the tree surgeon of gross malpractice.

However, it transpired that covenants in the development prevented homeowners from taking down any live trees, but permitted cutting of dead ones. A seething cityscape now filled the owner's picture window, without a single tree trunk to soften it. He had thousands of dollars worth of firewood, too. Perhaps killing them had been the point all along.

Within the parent science of gardening, arboriculture is the art of planting, cultivating, and managing trees and shrubs. Pruning can be defined as the process of cutting a plant with its health in mind. It should be done with great respect for the plant. Like surgeons, expert pruners know what to take and what to leave, and can explain what they're trying to do; this branch crosses over another, a heading cut here will make the tree send up branched supports instead of single shoots, to stiffen the lower branches, and everything out from this node is diseased and

must be lopped. All pruners may not use the arborist's language, but they understand the physiology of trees.

A tree is not a simple organism. Every single branch and leaf is in partnership and competition with others on the same tree. Pruning is one of those strange sciences, like bonsai, where what is taken away somehow enhances the structure of that which is left behind.

Pruning a tree is not a complicated art, but it requires more than just an idea, some tools, and a nice day. You must know what you are doing. The language of the expert pruner is filled with wonderful terms relevant to the work: candle, caliper, scaffold branching, radial branch spacing, water sprout, sucker, and central leader. If you don't know what those mean, put in a few hours of study before you haphazardly start shearing and lopping. The aim of pruning is to promote plant health, to restrict growth along desired lines, to repair wind damage, and to promote better flowers, fruit, and foliage. Done with love and knowledge, pruning can be a miracle cure for tree disease, or a magic way to make apples grow in a row along a fence for easy picking. I have seen an apple espalier done by a master pruner, and was duly boggled.

But ignorant treatment of trees is always horrible to behold. This is no longer the Oregon of my childhood. That place was mantled by towering forests where salmon ran thick in rivers and rills; even those were second-growth, but they were huge. Once, trees made a canopy from the coast to the Valley, a majestic and serene ecosystem, but over the last twenty years, the logs they became have been sent to the mills or exported. The shaved wreckage of hillsides was slash-burned, and then replanted in Hem-Fir, a hybrid designed for tree plantations. Flying over Oregon, pilots see only miles of quiltwork patches with geometrically straight lines of uncut timber, like the log walls of an abandoned fort.

In his first inaugural address, Thomas Jefferson wrote that Americans possessed "a chosen country with room enough for our descendants to the thousandth and thousandth generation." Less than ten generations later, most of the wilderness has vanished; not just the forests but the fauna as well, leaving only one species dominant.

I'm as responsible for this loss as anyone, directly and indirectly. As a carpenter

for the last twenty years, I've used "wood products" without giving forests much thought, hoping that they were limitless and inexhaustible. Now the clear-cuts stretch from horizon to horizon. I've never chained myself to a tree to protect virgin timber, as some of our neighbors have, or had to depend solely on logging jobs for a livelihood, like some of our other neighbors. The issues aren't simple, and they are powerfully divisive.

As I write this, loggers are taking down yet another section of forest within line of sight of our house. Their chainsaws sound like cattle bawling. At least they're real human lumberjacks earning a living, possibly our friends and neighbors, rather than the newest automated harvester. It seizes a tree in two lobster claws and cuts it off with a robotic saw on a swivel arm: a machine out of science fiction novels. The future has definitely arrived, and its name is Dystopia.

One summer, I worked in a cherry orchard as a fruit-picker and a tractor jockey. A lot of students worked in that orchard, most of them picking cherries from high three-legged ladders, but those who were trained to prune the trees stood on the highest rung, so to speak, of the hired help.

These pruning experts were an agricultural science major, a budding arborist, and a few high-school dropouts who had found a calling in the orchards. Most of them worked alone, one person to a cherry tree, but sometimes two would tackle a tree that needed much repair. Their tools included ladders, gloves, a sharp knife, a hand pruner, a good pair of loppers, a pole pruner (called a brashing saw in Britain), a short pruning saw, and most dangerous of all to life and limb, a chain saw. Their common quality was a love of trees. In my view, they all seemed to work by pure intuition, just diving into a tree and cutting where the spirit moved them. But that wasn't so; pruning styles and methods varied, but the outcomes were practically identical. Though pruned by different hands, every tree in that orchard was glowing with health, heavy with fruit, and structured perfectly.

Unfortunately, I worked in the summer and they worked in the winter, so I never learned to prune trees. Fortunately, Joy spent her first two working years in a Vermont apple orchard, so one of us has a clue. From her, I learned three main rules of pruning. First: Think about where you want a branch to be in three years. Second: If you're a shy pruner, be bold, and vice versa. Third: Never carry a chainsaw up in a tree. Everything else, Joy maintains, is just practice and details.

But practice makes perfect, and God is in the details. The point of pruning is to improve the condition of a tree: its current and future health, its structure and shape, and in an orchard, its ability to bear fruit. Good pruners examine a tree for a while before they prune, deciding what to cut and where. Ignorant pruners wade in with lopper and pruning saw to trim the tree like barbers, chopping branches almost randomly. Experienced pruners know enough to sterilize their tools between trees in a bucket of bleach and water; they know that the best way to treat a tree wound is almost never to staunch it with cosmetic pruning paint; they know the few exceptions, such as bark beetle infestation on an oak. Nonexperts lovingly daub each cut with tar or dark paint; but sunlight heats the wound and makes the wood crack.

Ignorance is not malice, but the result is the same. I read of one gardener who watched his wife cutting back rose bushes with loppers, so he went out in the back-yard and did the same to ten dwarf apple and pear saplings. One pear survived, almost by accident. His was not a malicious act, yet it had another earmark of vandalism: destruction and defacement. This crime got its name from the Vandals who sacked Rome, chopping up mosaics and tipping over statues, burning down olive groves and hacking at works of art. They did not believe they were doing an evil thing; just staying busy.

Think how many badly pruned trees you've personally seen. Gardening magazines sometimes run contests where people send in photos of bad pruning's ugly result, and they never lack entries; hundreds of maimed-tree pictures pour in. You can bet that no pruner meant to damage those trees, but the pure, raw ignorance of it is shocking. Lacking malice, this is not true vandalism, although it looks like it.

The most common mistake is topping: cutting off the trunk of a tree at the top. This can make the plant susceptible to disease or bug attack, or kill it altogether. The second most common error is to prune heavily after transplanting, supposedly to compensate for root loss.

When making a cut with loppers, keep the angle shallow, but not too flat or it won't shed water. You want a cut that will heal quickly, with as small a wound as possible. The bud nearest the cut becomes the new terminal, and the side buds grow faster. This is the tree's survival reaction. Loppers will cut up to two-inch

branches, but it's better to use a pruning saw on anything that size or bigger. To saw large branches, undercut the bottom of the branch at the collar (the zone at the base of the branch, protruding slightly from the trunk). Make a second cut on top, a little outboard from the bottom cut, and let the branch crack and fall. Finally, cut the stub cleanly, starting from the bottom cut.

The tree is not the only one in danger from unsafe pruning. If you have a good-size tree and any doubt about your tools or skills, hire an expert tree surgeon. A pole pruner can drop heavy branches on your head, but it is preferable to a high ladder from which you can fall; and should it touch a wire, a professional's fiberglass-handled pole pruner will not conduct high voltage from your hands to the ground, as a wood handle might and an aluminum handle will.

Reluctantly, I retired our oldest pair of loppers after a century of service. They just weren't cutting cleanly anymore, and the wood handles were ready to break. Our new loppers are by Sandvik, made in France with fiberglass handles and rubber grips. With care, these will last a hundred years. Our 8-point pruning saw is also new, with a fixed curved blade (safer than folding, some say) and a long leather scabbard that also holds a pair of secateurs. It replaced a bow saw that had always made unsatisfactory cuts.

The first time I pruned our apple tree, I was carefully following the textbook, thinking about each cut and working with clean new tools so oil would not contaminate the cuts. I snipped the small crossing branches, found the nodes correctly, lopped a bit of deadwood, and even buzzed out a twisted dead branch the size of my wrist. When Joy saw the tree, she congratulated me on technique, on the wisdom of disinfecting tools and not dressing the wounds, and she gave high marks to the overall job of cleanup. "The only thing is, there are still apples on the tree. You're supposed to wait until the tree goes dormant, the dead of winter or just before spring. Never in September."

The tree survived this incompetence, and will probably survive the incompetent pruner. Trees live a long time, even apple trees, unless they're cut down.

Coppicing, the archaic science of woodlot management on small farms, ensured that there would always be firewood and construction lumber growing behind homesteads. We know a man who logs his land only with horses. He has taken out trees every year for sale and firewood, but sparingly, shaping his forest as a pruner shapes one tree. He relies on a spring for his water supply, and the trees uphill from his watershed, he vows, will never be clear-cut.

We do not understand how ecosystems function, or how life in the topmost canopy of an old-growth forest is connected to the mycelium of mushrooms under the forest floor. We can prune genetic material but cannot predict how the gene-altered lifeform will adapt. The biosphere is a complex domain that seems to seek balance and equilibrium, right down to one terminal node of a single tree branch. All the evidence of our planet's current health points to a day of reckoning.

In Gray's Harbor, Washington, there once stood a virgin old-growth forest. It was one of the finest stands of uncut timber in North America. A section of original Doug Fir trunk looks like a building, it's so big, and Gray's Harbor had hundreds of thousands of them, a forest black and thick as the buffalo had been on the prairie, once upon a time. But the bison megaherd had been obliterated long before 1937, when the giants of Gray's Harbor were falling.

The creation of the Olympic National Forest halted the clear-cutting. When Franklin D. Roosevelt toured the Olympic Peninsula, he was lobbied heavily by the timber barons, who protested that a national forest would lock up the trees. But when Roosevelt gazed upon what was left of the magnificent forests of Gray's Harbor, moonscaped down to the bare dirt, he uttered these historic words: "I hope the son of a bitch who logged that is roasting in Hell."

There is no sight more terrible than ignorance in action.

◆

GOETHE

POTATO FORK

A Fork in the Disposal

Some gardeners say that newspaper makes acceptable compost. There's nothing much to it, other than cellulose and soy-based ink, with alphanumeric marks translating to scalding reports from those gardens of evil, big cities. Shred newspaper first and it will break down quickly, like manure. It makes the soil a little more acidic. But, I won't even use it for mulch. The temptation to read headlines underfoot would be too strong.

Like this one: Garbage disposals are once again legal in New York, thanks to improved city sewers. In the forced march of progress, the garbage disposal is a great leap backward because it sends the wrong message: Everything flushes.

A campaign for urban composting and vermiculture would be better news. Technology doesn't have to be a synonym for wasteful; it could mean worm barrels in skyscrapers, to break down tea bags, coffee grounds, stale bagels, and big apple cores into sweet soil for the flower beds of Central Park.

To save our little corner of the planet, I'll stick with a compost heap and garden fork. The day I buy and install a garbage disposal will be the Thirty-second of Never.

Proper composting means different things to different gardeners. Advocates of each method do not criticize one another, but a sniff means essentially the same thing. The many techniques of combining compost nutrients yield the same result if they work—rich, dark, loamy, manufactured but very natural-looking soil—but gardeners tend to become dogmatic about their composting formulae, methods, containers, and tools.

In the interest of world harmony, please try to be tolerant of other gardeners' composting practices, even if they're open to criticism. If you compost in rows of polished bins with a dash of commercial fertilizer to help them along, and the chap next door piles flyblown manure and crabgrass clippings into an unsightly

mound upon which he pees at night (an old gardener's trick for giving the pile a shot of starter nitrogen), chalk it up to the wonder of human diversity. He may be odd, but at least he's got the theory down.

As you might have guessed, my favorite composting tool is a garden fork. As a carpenter, I use one to remove old shingles from roofs and to loosen up topsoil when hand-digging footing trenches. It was Joy who first showed me the virtue of a garden fork in composting. A shovel won't dig deep enough in fresh working compost to turn it, although a trenching shovel works for making deep breathing-slots. The long, delicate tines of a pitchfork slide in easily and get stuck, but the garden fork stabs right into the mound and flops it over, ten pounds at a time, with a few brute-force twists. For those with more brains than brawn, the Walt Nicke catalog carries a compost aerator with tiny folding stainless-steel paddles, a canelike device that can be thrust in the pile and turned; this tool works, according to several of our neighbors, and saves much fork-flipping.

The garden fork is also called a potato fork, and vice versa. It's been around a long time, perhaps thousands of years. Few other tools will loosen up the ground in a potato patch as perfectly without ruining the tubers. At the very edge of your patch, push the fork in deeply at an angle, and push the handle down to the earth. The tines will bring up little troves of undamaged potatoes, from thumb-size nuggets to big bakers.

We have three versions of this tool: one fairly old fork, much weathered but still serviceable after fifty Oregon years; a newer version, made in England by Spear and Jackson with a split ash handle; and an elderly potato hook with a different design, its tines bent into an L-shape. All three forks get steady use during the growing season, and sometimes, when Joy, Ren, and I harvest potatoes, all three are in use at once.

Most of the time, I keep a fork somewhere near the compost heaps, for turning them when the mood strikes. We have three compost piles spaced around the garden. This is partly because one of the prime ingredients of the compost, manure, is in ample supply, but also because the grass must be mowed all year. We have to do something with all that manure and all those clippings, since we don't own an Insinkerator.

All the woody stuff must be chopped up into tiny pieces by hand, usually with a machete since we don't own a chipper/shredder, either. This means corn stalks, sunflower trunks, tree twigs, and the fibrous stems of most vegetables. Anything bigger gets burned in a pile at the end of the season and the ashes are scattered over the garden. This adds valuable potash to the soil.

A compost pile is, or should be, aerobically correct, with lots of ventilation. The trillions of soil microbes that do the work need to breathe. You can provide air mechanically by turning the pile, or put a perforated six-inch ABS pipe down the center and build your pile around it, or layer some sticks into the pile and pull them out after a couple of weeks. You can aerate with special tools, but aerate you must. If you ensure that grass clippings or other easily matted material are mixed with straw or leaves, you'll avoid suffocating your compost, which is announced by a revolting and memorable anaerobic stench.

Compost tumblers work so well because the aeration is complete and uniform, making the process go even faster. The contents are sealed inside a ventilated tub made of UV-stabilized plastic, with interior baffles and a hatch for removal when the compost is ready; a few turns of the crank every day is all that's needed. But when they're full, turning might be difficult for anyone who isn't fairly able-bodied. Alternatively, you can make bins or boxes with wood-slat sides, stack concrete blocks, weave wire into huge baskets, perforate metal or plastic drums, or invent new methods that are worth patenting. Composting options are endless, and although it's an old science, composting is still in its infancy in twentieth-century America.

But it's getting popular. The number of commercial composters in the state has tripled in the last five years; Portland recycles three-fourths of its yard waste now. Ten years ago, it was one-fifth. In an item from *The Oregonian*: Commercial composters who run big-time operations (fueled by spoiled fruit, yard debris from all over Portland, and other organic offal) have hit a snag. Land-use laws keep them out of rural areas, and they can't expand in urban areas because of odor problems. Business has tripled in the last five years.

Compost recipes need four main ingredients: carbon, nitrogen, oxygen, and water. The carbon is supplied by leaves, sawdust, wood ash, grass clippings, or shredded

vegetable matter; the nitrogen by manure, seaweed, and garbage such as fruit peels and vegetable scraps. The ideal ratio is about 25 parts carbon to one part nitrogen, according to most compost experts, but I ignore proper ratios and just layer fresh horse manure, old sawdust bedding from the barn, soiled straw from the chicken coop, gopher mound dirt, and grass clippings. Thin layers ensure a more complete mix, and I turn it every three days or every other week, whichever comes last. Even this clumsy, unscientific method gives us smoking hot compost piles; the trick, I believe, is complete aeration, not a perfect mix of carbon and nitrogen.

You can boost your pile with municipal compost, often given free to city residents or sold cheaply by the bag, and some agencies will rate the percentages of nitrogen, phosphorus, and potassium for you. There are proprietary formula compost activators such as Quick Return (called "QR" in England, where they swear by it); one packet treats a ton. According to some, peat moss works great for holding moisture in the compost, although we don't use it. Worm castings will nicely aerate the pile and improve its ability to retain nutrients, and you can either add worms or wait for them to come. Zoos sell elephant manure (in bags) for a touch of the exotic.

But don't put meat, fish, eggs, oils, or fats on the top of the pile because they attract flies and vermin. You can leave these out, or bury them two feet deep in some recondite corner of your garden and start a compost pile there.

I have no qualms whatsoever about adding spoiled milk or milk products; they increase the calcium quotient, and when poured into a hole in the pile's center, there's no smell. You can include dust from vacuum cleaner bags if you choose, but not if it's full of nylon carpet yarn. Some composters add human hair from barbershops; just thinking about it makes something feel like it's stuck in the back of my throat. Omit ash from coal fires, and burning cinders from any type of fire. Compost can ignite and burn like peat.

There are those who compost animal wastes. My feeling is that dog doo is unacceptable even on the lawn, let alone in our garden. Some people empty their cat litter boxes on their compost heap. Call it an irrational prejudice; even if microbes and nematodes break it down into its component molecules, I don't want atoms that have been inside a cat to go inside a tomato and thence, in time, inside me. All forms of dog, cat, or parakeet night soil should be buried for many years before we see it again; not including rabbit poop, which is excellent for composting and worm farming.

Do not add sawdust from treated wood or cedar, diseased plants, and in my own lone and miserable opinion, which will be disputed as heresy by many gardeners, fresh green weeds. Whap, flutter, crash: hear the sound of many gardeners slapping their foreheads and throwing this book across the room. As stated, gardeners hold strong opinions on composting methods.

Weeds should be perfect candidates for compost. They are organic, handy, and plentiful. But identifying weeds is like picking your own wild table mushrooms: if you know for sure, you're safe. However, too many gardeners have tossed in privet, ivy vines, creeping grasses like (but not limited to) quackgrass, sheep sorrel, bindweed, oxalis, and dandelion plumes, and these gardeners who thought they were safe are now sorry.

My motto is, Do not trust a dead weed. Although compost can get hot enough at the center to cook weed seeds and kill roots, some will inevitably escape, and then your compost can sprout vicious, pernicious, invasive weeds. Some gardeners have managed to make perfectly good compost using weeds like Canadian thistle, but since thistles retain enough moisture to go to seed even when pulled, how they did it is a mystery.

I let weeds dry in the hot sun and then burn them to ashes, before they go near our compost. However, many gardeners toss weeds right on the pile and never have a lick of trouble. A friend of ours cannot believe that I don't add fresh weeds to compost, and he thinks I'm being unnecessarily paranoid, although we agree on omitting cat box additives. Maybe I'm wrong and green-weed composters are right.

If you're going to make a compost pile, start with a patch of bare ground that's convenient to your garden, if not centrally located. Plan for easy access by wheelbarrow or pickup truck, and within reach of a garden hose. Give it as much surface area as you can spare, since a heap has to have center mass to work, and it shrinks down as it cooks. Pile it high and aerate it often. The outside layer insulates the pile, allowing high temperatures to build up in the middle. As the pile is turned, all material spends some time decomposing in the center.

A few composting manuals say full shade is better than full sun because you don't want compost to dry out, but if you cover it with a tarp, there's some instant shade, and rain won't leach out the good stuff. Some gardeners keep their heaps in the same spot forever. We tend to move our piles around, to fertilize and renew fallow beds, and fork the compost frequently.

Off the compost heap, the garden fork finds other jobs. Incidentally, it's the perfect hand tool for a job called "tilthing," the verb form of tilth and the worst possible way to make soil: labor-intensive, murder on your vertebrae, unreasonably dirty, and difficult to pronounce without sounding impaired.

To tilth, smash clods of broken-up dirt with a swinging action somewhere between golf and baseball, as follows: bring the fork up and smash it down at a sideways angle to break up the clods into crumbly dirt. Try it for an hour, but not with a light spading fork, or you'll beat it to death.

This is an old, old method of breaking soil, and will come back in vogue only if civilization collapses. Whoever invented this technique obviously didn't have access to a tiller or even livestock, but whoever revived that word must have been trying to punish the English language. It's an Anglo-Saxon cough, spoken as if your tongue wanted to go outside and play. Tilth that thoil in the hot thun if it pleatheth you, then relax in the coolth under a tree. Or use a tiller.

Blessed be agriculture! There is life in the ground.

◆

CHARLES DUDLEY WARNER

SECATEURS

Winter lasts forever, a nesting time that seems to have no end, but once the pink days of summer start, they flit by like swallows. In a climate where it rains at least once a month, we reach into those sunny days, pulling their warmth inside us, storing them against the time when we'll need them most. We open our senses; it is a time to live. If there are troubles, they should be endured with gratitude for the gift of light, as each sunrise begins a new day.

This morning was filled to the brim with beauty. I was standing on a ladder by our front gate, clipping the dense overgrowth of branches away with secateurs and ebrancheurs, the evergreen boughs still wet from last night's rain. Clouds were rolling off to the east. Dawn began in soft shades of carmine and gold that spread into a fat ellipse of golden light; when the sun pushed the clouds back like blue and purple petals, all it lacked was French horns. It was good to be alive in the glow of such a marvelous morning, even if I can't see all its wonders clearly.

There has been something in my eye for over a month now. A beamlike mote seems to be stuck in the iris, despite frequent lavings with eye drops. The pain comes and goes, making my eyes water all the time. It's a little reminder to practice what I always preach. For certain nonconstruction jobs, such as sharpening tools or pruning, always wear eye protection.

Out of my good eye, I drink in the marigolds and roses of our garden, the green of the hills around. Joy is up early, gathering flowers for a wedding; this is a day to be savored, a celebration.

It was on a summer day like this that my father passed away at home. It was not a very long dying, and the angels of Hospice made it as comfortable as it could be. His family surrounded him, keeping watch as if we could keep death from getting past. The days moved slowly then. Mac used his remaining time well, saying

his farewells with love and long conversations. And then one morning, he slipped away just after dawn.

All the rivers run into the sea. All the flowers return to the earth. We held a small memorial service by his favorite river, casting ashes on the water, saving some back to sprinkle upon our flower beds. His ashes were divided among those he loved, poured solemnly into small yogurt containers, a touch he would have appreciated. At twilight, my brother held out the last ladle of gray powder: "Anyone want more Mac?"

When Joy and I began training for certification as Hospice volunteers, we pruned and thinned the old rose bushes that grew wild in our backyard. Hopefully, we planted more flower beds in the thin and rocky soil. They have flourished with unexpected strength, and I believe the secret is potash.

Today we have a wedding to attend. The McKenzie-Rivers are renewing their vows at the community center, and the call went out last night from the Women's Circle flower committee: More flowers. Thousands of flowers. The center should be filled to the rafters with flowers.

Joy is already cutting them with her new secateurs, a fancy French word for "cutters," like calling loppers "ebrancheurs." But *secateurs* is a prettier word, and shorter than *pruning shears*. There is something meditative, almost a ritual, about cutting flowers instead of picking them. A tool slows the hand, making us dwell on the life of flowers, and the flowers of life itself in our small town.

A hundred years ago, Whatsun began as a logging town on a plateau at the crest of the coast range. It had sawmills, saloons, churches, bawdy houses, smithies, stables, and one general store, the only commercial structure that remains. When the forests were cut, most of the people moved on, and the town dried up.

And thus it stayed over the long years of the Depression, the empty hills growing back their coat of trees, the land moving through the seasons. Deer nibbled the daffodils in front of old abandoned farms, and the salmon returned to their spawning grounds as they always had. Decades passed.

In the sixties, Whatsun underwent a sea change when waves of California's young fled the madding sunshine, looking for something they could not quite name. They

came north, living in buses and tepees and domes, startling the old-timers who still logged and raised cattle. One ninety-year-old resident, who had seen the Native Americans dwindle away, said this migration was like tribes gathering for a celebration: buckskin, beads, hair, paint, and feathers. A mighty pony-herd of painted Volkswagens rumbled in, year after year, questing for a place to park forever.

They found the mountain first, of course, and that was their landmark. Mary's Mountain had been holy to all the tribes who lived in sight of it; they called it *Tscha Tamanwi*, "the high place of the spirits." Their young seekers of visions spent the night on its side, learning to listen to the world. The first French trappers who saw it fell to their knees, naming it after their Holy Mother, and drank its purifying waters. By any name, the mountain was still the mountain and was still and ever holy. Every person who lives in Whatsun has been to the mountain, and most of us have spent the night. It is our beacon.

A diversity of lifestyles does not come into harmony all at once. Gardens were planted in season, and it was not rare to see a hairy person holding a hoe with feathers taped to its handle talking over a fence with a cattle rancher sitting on a tractor. There was friction in the early days, even combustion, fueled by the fierce energy of the times. But time passed, and slowly the great sifting process began. Soon children were born, and the women began to make quilts.

A community gives depth and strength to its members, to celebrate passages, to bring neighbors into kinship, to heal wounds. Privacy must be honored, but without the company of others, winter would be dark indeed. Our rituals and gatherings bind us together: quilting bees, poker games, barn dances, marriages, baby showers, and memorial services. There is a summer festival. In winter, Whatsun holds a talent show.

Country life has drawbacks, but in Whatsun, we take care of our own and look out for everyone else's. None go hungry. No tear falls without a hand to wipe it, if company is needed; if solitude, neighbors protect the space. Midwives sit with expectant mothers, friends sit with the dying. A sense of collective history weaves through the fabric of families, the clans and friends and neighbors, interlinked by a thousand things. There is a volunteer-run preschool, and the children who live here grow up knowing one another. Perhaps the primary function of community is to raise healthy children.

In the afternoon, five cars arrive, full of women carrying baskets and secateurs, water vases, ribbons to tie bouquets. Joy goes with them, and the Whatsun Wolvettes lope off in full force, cruising the mountains in search of more flowers. What a movie scene it would make: this pack of wild women bonded in rural sisterhood, making the rounds of all their backyards first, and then running through far-off meadows sprinkled with daisies and lupine. The aerial camera pulls back, rising to take in the hilly countryside, the bright day of the greening earth, and the motley fleet of flower cars rushing toward the Whatsun Center.

The center was once an old church, built high on a hill overlooking Whatsun. It has been desanctified and made into a hall, its steeple removed to avoid confusion. But the pews remain. In those early days, young hippies on tractors and old loggers on Caterpillars moved the center to its current location in the middle of town. The whole event was captured on film for posterity. Thirty years have passed since moving day, and this building has been hallowed by all the gatherings under its rooftree.

It is time to gather for the wedding. As the center fills with neighbors, the young hover in a little knot of nose rings, black leather, and angstful looks; how many times we have told them, patiently, that they don't have to dress like refugees. But who could have known that posterity would find those faded photographs, proudly framed on the south wall, to be so hilarious? They crowd around the pictures, pointing and snickering at do-rag bandannas, keep-on-trucking bell-bottoms, the peace medallions, and the Earth flags, ha-ha. When they run the community someday, may their children videotape them.

The wedding takes place at dusk, amid flowers. Surrounded by bouquets of wild iris and marigold, late daisies and snapdragons, hollyhocks and foxglove, the bride and groom meet, touching hands. The preacher raises his hands. Silence descends, the pews are filled. The center is a church once more. In the presence of God and all their neighbors, Spud and Windy renew their vows. Afterward, with violins and guitars, the reception takes place outside on the lawn. One of the gifts is a quilt made by the whole community, even the children. Many eyes leak, including mine, but it is only something in my eye.

When the wedding is over and the cleanup begins, Joy takes some of the flowers to her Hospice patient in another town. The first rule of Hospice is confidentiality, so nothing can be said about this person except that she particularly loves

roses and probably weddings. Passing over is the end of pain, but deeper hurts have not been addressed, and there is no time for language. Flowers mean acceptance. Once a person has reached the final stage of accepting his or her pending death, a sense of peace seems to fill the dying room, like the essence of flowers.

Gardens teach us many things about life and death. The first green shoots carry the promise of their own completion. In the circular sweep of seasons, we see the circumference of our own lives. Summer weather lingers on as if it were here to stay, but always after comes autumn, harvest, and sleep. Without winter, spring would lose its sweetness.

Ages ago, the earth was bare of flowers. Upon a day, there were gymnosperms loose in the world; and as Loren Eiseley wrote, those tiny flowers changed the face of the planet. By doing so, they made the human race possible. It is a small payment on this debt to plant and nurture them, to ensure that flowers will be here tomorrow, and for tomorrows yet to come. They remind us of what is important.

Flowers may beckon towards us, but they speak toward heaven and God.

◆

HENRY WARD BEECHER

WATERING CAN

Water Everywhere

It's a pretty day, the sun beating down with as much sincerity as July can muster. I'm watering the flowers in the side yard at the end of fifty feet of hose, pretending to be an elephant, when I notice the Tiger waddling over toward the garden. He was named for his regal attitude toward humans, not his color scheme: black coat, white nose and underbelly. His entire daily workload consists of hunting songbirds, sleeping on windowsills, and refrigerator worship. He glides along with the fluid grace of a killer whale until he comes to the freshly tilled earth. He sniffs it. In the manner of cats, he considers it briefly, and deems it suitable.

That's cat-gratitude for you. This morning, even before coffee, I fed him, gave him a full body massage, let him out, let him back in, and let him back out. His indoor litter latrine is spotless, courtesy of his own personal Gandhi, me.

Looks like time for a little aversion therapy. He's in range. Must wait until it is absolutely certain that Tiger has mistaken our garden for his catbox annex. When training companion animals, timing of negative stimuli is vital.

He digs, he adjusts his feet for comfortable support, he arches his tail just so, looking as relaxed and natural as a police car parked by a doughnut shop. He closes his eyes; maybe he is solving Fermat's Last Theorem. His ears have barely begun to flatten when a stream of water descends on him, a sudden monsoon in the middle of a sunny day. From a squatting start, Tiger warps off in pussy-cat hyperdrive, an astounding display of speed for a cat whose body so resembles a panda's in color and shape.

That was swell. The only thing that would make it better is automation. There's a new product on the market called a Scarecrow, which connects a hose to a motion sensor to keep critters out of the garden. A minor twinge of conscience about hosing the cat, and then I rationalize that cats have dignity to spare, more than they need. And far too much leisure time compared to the big monkey.

All summer, we'll be hauling water to our plants, a lot of it by hand. Gardens should not drink so much, but they do. Normally we get abundant rain before and after the growing season, but far too little during; this summer has been a little wetter than last, but we still have to irrigate. Over four months' time, thousands of gallons of our favorite mineral will disappear into the thirsty beds, rows, mounds, and tubs.

Say what you will, but water is unique in the catalog of garden additives, and precious as gold in many cultures. Of the world's total water supply, most is salt water or ice. Maybe 10 percent is still clean enough to drink or water gardens, and this fraction diminishes daily due to pollution.

St. Francis, that lover of Nature, called it "our sister Water, so sweet, so fresh, so pure." We're thinking of setting up a garden shrine to the saint of Assisi, perhaps near the Green Man, to bless the garden and to protect rabbits and raccoons from an unthinking lethal response when I catch them chewing vegetables.

For the most part, we use hoses to move water. Last spring, after much prompting from Joy, I put another faucet on the south side of the house, and one inside the greenhouse. This entailed diving down the pantry hatchway with a sack of tools, including a clean rag and a book of matches. It was supremely unpleasant. The space between kitchen joists and earth is a little less than two feet, shrouded in filth and spider webs. Beady rat and spider eyes were staring at the back of my neck, when they weren't twinkling in the dark beyond the light's circle. I heard furry shuffling back by the crawl hole, my only avenue of escape.

"I'm just visiting," I told all the creatures of darkness. "You don't bother me, I won't bo . . ." A dry rustle, right behind me. When something wet and twitchy sniffed my nape, I screamed the Lord's full legal name. It was only the cat, come to explore. "Get lost, Tiger! You hairy fathead, you scared the hell out of me." He slouched away to hunt.

I cruised along on my elbows to the nearest pipe, a place with all the elbow room of a walrus in a coffin. Flipping over on my back, I then cut the pipe, collected a gallon of water in the puss, wiped it off my face with the rag, and started sweating the copper tee-joint—acid flux and hot solder dripping past my ear, propane flame occasionally licking at the wooden members.

Finally, I connected the new pipe and slithered back into daylight, feeling and looking inhuman. Then I had to go back under and fetch the cat. Never again. But now we have hoses that can reach any plant on our property; now we can make them wet, because that's all a hose does.

Sure, hoses are convenient, and great as water mortars for bombarding cat sappers in the wire. The brass nozzle will put gallons of water anywhere I want it and produce a fine spray with a twist. We couldn't garden without a hose. We use five all summer long. All sorts of great nozzles and wands screw on the ends, and they'll shape the water into a tight stream or a misting fog, and everything in between.

But I submit, without any scientific proof, that when you water a plant with a watering can, it is a more personal service of love, and perhaps received as such. I'm not entirely sure what I mean by this, nor am I completely comfortable with it. This belief of mine, when I think it through, means that I accept the fact that plants are conscious; maybe not self-aware in the human sense, but self-aware nonetheless. Plants go to sleep, plants wake up; they digest and excrete; they live and they die; they adapt to conditions and respond to stimuli, just like me.

Wait, what am I saying? If plants are conscious, that means weeds are conscious. The karmic implications of that one don't bear thinking about. Forget I mentioned it. Hose everything and don't lose any sleep worrying about such New Age claptrap.

But if you have an open mind, read about Findhorn, the Scottish gardening community. Or *The Secret Life of Plants* by Peter Tompkins and Christopher Bird. Or Judith Handelsman's *Growing Myself.* These books explore some of the mysticism of the plant kingdom, and raise some interesting questions about the nature of consciousness. Talking to plants is slowly becoming conventional wisdom among gardeners. The next step, some would say, is listening to plants.

We talk to our vegetables, trees, and flowers, most often when we're using the watering can, almost never when running a hose or setting up sprinklers. Dribbling water onto their little heads by hand feels like a silent ritual, prayer by action, to honor the spirit of life that makes flowers and people blossom, tomatoes and children grow and get big. Maybe that's what I mean.

You'd think the watering can would be obsolete this late in the twentieth century, except perhaps for window boxes. But no. Joy wets down the greenhouse plants and all the tubbed shrubbery on the deck with a can, sometimes adding a drop or two of liquid fertilizer. The watering can duplicates a light rain, sprinkling out from the holes in the rose, as the business end is called. Ours is a faithful old steel can with a brass rose, perhaps made just before or right after the Second World War; there would have been little brass available until that was over.

It must have been an incredible time to be alive. Those years were the last time in American history that this nation actively practiced conservation of raw materials. Joy keeps her seeds in a small green grocery bag made of cloth; when she found it, there was a leather book of wartime ration stamps inside. The bag bears the painted motto, "Eat Nutritional Food," apparently because "US needs us strong!" (Sloganeering has come a long way since then.) It is smaller than the average paper grocery sack today, probably because we have to carry home more product packaging than in the old days of nostalgic memory. Even fresh water is packaged these days, with expensive designer water lining the shelves of supermarkets. There are eight million cubic miles of fresh water in lakes, rivers, and clouds, which seems like a lot, but it represents half a percent of all the water in the world. All the rest is undrinkable. It's something to think about when you're watering a plant.

Our watering can holds about three gallons, coincidentally the capacity of our largest rubber bucket. The water goes on our houseplants and garden from a variety of hoses, buckets, and watering cans. We spray our indoor greenery weekly with water to humidify them, using a recycled plastic spray bottle.

If you want a watering can with some class, the same one found in the finest English gardens, buy the Haws. This company is Britain's premier watering can manufacturer, if you can imagine the concept, and they've made a science of watering can design. Their newest model, fully balanced whether full or empty, is fitted with a nondrip oval rose, cleverly facing up, and with an extra-long neck that can reach the highest plants on our greenhouse shelves.

This is the pinnacle of watering-can design, and if you have to ask about the price, you probably aren't worthy to own one. Stick to the Haws traditional can, the same type Peter Rabbit hid inside. Sizes range from three gallons down to one pint.

We've put one on the List for purchase someday because our watering can has

already sprung its first leak. As a homage to the vanished age of tinkers, I fixed it the old-fashioned way: first I drilled the leak point to make a circular quarter-inch hole, and then I installed a nut and bolt with rubber washers on both sides. Once tightened, the bolt sealed the leak, until the next one. Galvanized steel lasts about sixty years, so it's nearing the end of its life.

Water is an issue in the West, especially for western gardeners. Either we get too much at the wrong time, or too little when it's needed; winter floods leach valuable nutrients from the topsoil all winter, drought bakes our tomatoes in the summer. Even after one of the soggiest winters on record, several of our neighbors have run their wells dry this year. In the news, global weather patterns seem to be a little shaky. Each summer, it gets a little hotter. Perhaps Gaia is trying to tell us something.

This culture is extravagant with water, to use a euphemism for criminal waste. Every day, another gallon of pure water goes down a toilet, hoses off an automobile, or is used to dilute plutonium soup. Everywhere, groundwater that had been pure and potable for the last million years is now swarming with giardia, coliform bacteria, dioxin, PCBs, insecticides, fertilizers, phosphates, and lead. Shaded riverbanks where moose and humans could drink from the same river's edge (if not at the same time) now sport toilet paper mills and outflow tubes. Hamburger chains proliferate; every pound of hamburger takes 2,500 gallons of water to produce. And in parts of southern California, treated sewage liquid must be pumped directly into underground aquifers, since without recycled water there wouldn't be enough to slake California's thirst. When future historians examine what we've done, they won't say, "That culture sure had a deep respect for water." By then, the consciousness of rivers may be an established scientific fact.

We water our garden with well water, a rural luxury, keeping the plants moist enough to thrive without draining our well. So far, it's never happened; the waterbearing clay shale of our home aquifer restores itself every winter, and we're careful not to be too lavish with water during the hot months.

However, that's when gardens need daily watering. Even slight moisture stress can harm the quality of lettuce, which turns bitter, and many others. Squash is smart enough to curl its leaves to curb moisture loss, but given dry conditions, you'll get woody, tasteless summer squash. We considered a drip irrigation system, but the tangle of pipes and hoses makes weeding and soil cultivation harder. Next year, we may wind up pumping it up from the river.

Spot watering with a watering can, however, wastes virtually no liquid through evaporation. The water sinks right down in the thirsty soil beside the roots. Every drop goes a little further.

A note of caution: There are times to water the garden immediately, and times when it is best not to water it at all. Joy explained this to me long ago: Morning is the proper time to turn on the sprinklers and douse with the watering can; if you wet down your vegetable garden just as night is coming on, thousands of slugs and one million viruses naturally gravitate thither. Everything else wants to get warm and dry when the sun goes down, but such is the evil of the forces marshaled against gardens that many prefer a Lovecraftian environment of wet, dark, and slime. So the only time we water at night is during our Full Moon Slug Hunt.

Joy sometimes says, and usually while she's tilting the watering can, that plants can feel love. It might go even further. They may feel it for us.

A tomato does not communicate with a tomato, we believe. We could be wrong.

◆

GUSTAV ECKSTEIN

PITCHFORK

Savage Garden

Music in a garden is not a bad idea. As a carpenter, I spent twenty years shunning radios as needless distractions, but when gardening or working outside, the right kind of music lifts spirits and makes hard work joyful. Plants seem to like Bach's *Magnificat*, Vivaldi's *The Four Seasons*, and Pachelbel's Canon in D. I like rock and roll, Joy plays quite a bit of jazz, and Serenity's musical tastes include none of the above.

This last wasn't a problem until I ran a power line out to the barn and put a radio where the chickens could hear it. It's increased their egg production, and the horse doesn't mind listening to Mozart or Beethoven all day. The storm began when I tuned the radio to an oldies station today, for something to listen to while I helped Ren clean out her horse's small barn. Every Saturday, we clean it out together, whether we're speaking or not.

I sense a strange disturbance in the Force. Seemingly overnight, the apple of my eye has become a teenager. Serenity is thirteen, a difficult number, and the child I once dandled on my knee is rapidly becoming a young woman. I recall cutting her cord, long ago, under this very rooftree.

"What are they wailing about?" Ren asks, they being Crosby, Stills, Nash, and Young, playing on the radio. I explain that they're upset about unarmed students shot dead in 1970 on their own campus. She shrugs: history, so what. Thirteen is a storm-tossed age at best, and the nineties are a hard time to come of age. When I was thirteen, the television never dared whisper a hell or damn, let alone the clearly enunciated filth that comes out of its speaker now. Drugs in school were aspirin; gangs meant the Jets and Sharks dancing in a school production of *West Side Story*.

Apropos of nothing: "Dad. Are you going to buy me a car when I'm sixteen?" This is progress; we're dialoguing. To support her case, Ren lists off a few dozen friends whose fathers have made this commitment, or had it extorted from them.

At this age, a car is almost the last thing we want her to fixate on. A boyfriend is the last thing. "In all likelihood, honey, no. Owning a car is a big respons—" But she's already stopped listening. Parenting a teenager, apart from qualifying one for canonization, often puts the hapless parent on the horns of an agricultural dilemma: whether to raise a fresh kid or a spoiled one.

Ten minutes of silence ensue. I jockey the wheelbarrow into position once more, clearing my throat. "You know, pitchforks used to be made entirely of wood." Figure it's time to say something.

"Really?" Ren mutters, in the teen tone that means *Really couldn't care less.* She goes on raking with her own special manure rake, pointedly rejecting my tool of choice, the pitchfork.

It's an admirable tool with many uses. Surely you have seen villagers surrounding the castle of Baron Frankenstein, waving torches and farming tools. So you cannot have missed the foremost defensive implement in the hands of the mob folk. Throughout the ages, common peasants with farming tools have never been unarmed; in fact, a soldier with a sword had better watch his mouth around a peasant with a scythe. By contrast, the pitchfork works like a foil, not a saber; it is for deflecting attacks, not slashing off heads. Lancers on horseback sometimes found this out. A hayfork can catch and deflect a lance, and it turns armored horsemen into broken pedestrians. Sometimes a pitchfork is a way of maintaining an open and equal dialogue.

"Yeah. They split an ash pole at the end, two cuts for three tines, and steamed it there until they could spread the tines and carve them—"

"Wheelbarrow's full," she says, chopping off further historical woodworking information. I haul it off to the compost pile, fighting the urge to quietly yodel along with Neil Young. That would just irritate her further.

She was raised in our little New Age community, a more stable environment than her parents ever saw. We were careful to impart one of our most cherished family values: Question Authority. We must have had something else in mind than what inevitably happened, but she learned the lesson. Ren was always a direct child; only now has she learned to tread the edge of her power. We've tried to help her find her own self-respect, balanced with a healthy respect for others.

After dumping the wheelbarrow, I use the pitchfork to layer on some straw, and I hose the compost down. Back to the barn for some more interaction. There are no conversational openings in the enormous silence between us. Otherwise, I could tell her that the first time I used a pitchfork was on my uncle's farm, at about her age, to gather up loose hay and feed it to cattle. At one time, until the hay-baler was invented, pitchforking was a science. Farmers learned to stack hay with the stems in each layer perpendicular to the ones above and below, so the haystack wouldn't shift. There are no more haystacks, but the pitchfork remains unparalleled as a manure tool.

The time has come to talk of unpleasant things, those aspects of the garden that do not involve flowers, ducks, or bunnies. That-which-happens is not very nice at the moment of production, but after it has aged, it becomes gold—at least for gardeners.

Manure is organic, pure and uncorrupted by artificial chemicals as the driven snow. Fresh manure bursts with amazing odors and draws flies, but eventually it breaks down and only smells objectionable, instead of terrible. But here is the mixture of this blessing: manure is an excellent fertilizer for the garden. It is so rich in nutrients that it cannot be applied immediately to gardens, which tend to surfeit and die of too much of this good thing. It is teeming with pathogenic organisms, but air and sunlight eventually thin them out, incidentally reducing the smell. At some point, it is no more filthy than good garden soil. Manure works best after it rots.

Well-rotted manure: Drop this innocuous phrase at a cocktail party, and watch all heads snap up. Or just say "green manure," which is nothing more than a nice sweet cover crop, tilled under in the spring. Whatever you say about the topic, it will not sound nice. The language of ordure is frankly unpleasant. Therefore, in the interest of clean language describing a dirty subject, this garden additive will henceforth be called, universally, "manure." Feel free to substitute the snappier, four-letter word wherever you deem it appropriate.

"Doonka plonk, dootie; Old man, take a look at my—"

"Dad. Must you?" Ren hates Neil Young, fathers who sing to themselves, and all sixties music. Who knew?

"—my, uh, life. Sorry."

"I mean, it was bad enough on the radio." She has filled the wheelbarrow again. I wheel it off.

This pitchfork is about fifty years old, at a guess. It's outlasted all the others, but when it breaks, I'll have to get another one. They're not common in garden supply catalogs or garden stores because there's not a lot of demand for them. But they're perfect for some gardening jobs; when Joy weeds, she tosses them onto the lawn, and I come along behind with the pitchfork and wheelbarrow to gather up the wilted weeds. I can't think of a better tool, either, for spreading straw and leaf mulch. Sometimes Joy runs it across the rows of baby carrots to thin them; it does less damage than a rake. Which reminds me . . .

"Did I ever tell you about the time—" That's how far I get before Ren explains that she came out here to clean her horse's barn, not listen to my reminiscences. Well, the wheelbarrow is full again, so I've got an excuse to remove my execrable presence.

I know why she's really upset. Last night at the health club, two husky nineteen-year-old hormone-drenched werewolves were hitting on her when I came to pick her up. Apparently she had augmented her true age by about three years; in the course of the we-gotta-go conversation, I disabused them. It was subtly done, the merest mention. But it was the wrong thing to do, apparently.

Joy was horrified when I told her. "You didn't."

"I did. Was it wrong?"

"Absolutely. You embarrassed her. Don't be so overprotective."

Recently, I find myself gripped by an awful nostalgia for the long-gone days when she could find delight in *Goodnight, Moon* and the tales of Beatrix Potter. Last year, she let me read *Politically Correct Bedtime Stories*, and I realized with a kind of keening heartbreak that, oh my little child, those happy days of reading stories to her were over.

This is the awful age at which fathers of daughters begin to look wary whenever the topic turns to the animal known as "boy." Recently, specimens of this creature have begun to lurk about the fringes of my life, and I've had to keep my eye on a few. "He's cute," Ren will say about this one or that one. Or, "He's fine," which means approximately the same thing.

I have a plan. When the age of dating arrives, about fifteen unless we turn Amish, none of her first boyfriends will arrive without noting the pitchfork in my hands. They should unconsciously associate me with the Devil incarnate, someone capable of anything, unstable to the max. Before they try something funny, they will ask themselves: What might the old man do to me?

But first, I'll put them at ease, lull them into relaxing, followed by a few tidbits of conversation on book research: "What am I working on? A compendium of medieval torture methods." A datum or two like that inscribed on the hard drive of their libidos will help any young lad find the strength to embrace abstinence.

A kindly neighbor gave us a bit of advice, long ago: Horse-crazy is better than boy-crazy. "You get that girl a horse, and you can rest easy for an extra year or two. When they're developin' and all at that age, and they got a horse, what do they need a boy for?" Sound country wisdom, we thought.

Ren's first small pony, Silver, has moved on to other pastures. In his place, a large roan mare now lives in the barn. Her breed is mostly Arabian, meaning she's high-spirited and has a mind of her own, like her owner.

Absently, I light a cigarette, standing in the hay-filled barn where I am never, never supposed to smoke. Suddenly, Ren has much to say to me. Don't I have any sense of responsibility about my addictions? And so forth. After that, things go to hell rather quickly.

In the evening, Joy and I talk. "I'm sure it's nothing," she says. I'm rubbing my temples, trying to fend off a blinding headache. "She's just mad. She'll get over it."

"My God, it was a nightmare. We're done cleaning the barn, and out of the blue she starts—*picking* on me."

Joy does this thing with her eyebrows sometimes. One of them goes way up.

"Okay, she demanded to know when I was going to quit smoking." There, it's out.

Joy nods. "So, when *are* you going to quit smoking?"

"Don't you start. This year."

Ren comes inside, through the kitchen, on her way to her room. "Hi, Mom." She looks right through me.

"Ren? Look, about last night, I want to apologize—"

"Mom, do you hear something? Because I certainly don't hear anything." Exit, with flourishes.

Joy and I exchange the timeless look of parents, a glance that is bemused, weary, compassionate, hopeful.

"She's thirteen," Joy explains. "Just be patient with her. Thirteen is hard."

Tell me about it.

To create a little flower is the labor of ages.

◆

WILLIAM BLAKE

HAT

Secrets in the Shade

My favorite summer gardening hat began life as a Panama, but it's been worn and punched into the shape of something Steve McQueen might have worn in an old cowboy picture. Like many gardening hats, it's made from palm straw, which is light on the head and lets in the breezes.

The first straw hats in America were made in 1798 by a Rhode Island girl named Betsey Metcalf. She was twelve years old when she plaited oat straw into hats and sold them for a dollar apiece. Most fashionable hats of those days were made of beaver fur and cost ten times as much, but they weren't comfortable. Farmers and gardeners beat a path to Betsey's door, and the rest is history.

When I was nine, I asked my Uncle Bob why he always wore a hat. His farm was the only place I felt at ease in my cowboy hat. No one ever laughed if I wore it there. In fact, all my cousins wore hats just like it. It was during one of those childhood summer holidays, when we drove from Oregon to Iowa for weeks of immersion in the Midwestern ethic. There I noticed that agriculturalists on any scale, from thousand-acre farmers to backyard gardeners, all wore hats, caps, or bonnets.

My uncle's hat was typical: stained with sweat and dirt, it appeared to be a locomotive engineer's cap made of pillow ticking, high crowned with a short bill, blue and white striped fabric overlaid with brown dust. My aunt washed it every night. I had never seen him without it when he left the house. He took it off for lunch, but it went on the moment he stepped outdoors.

Uncle Bob was an Iowa farmer, a man of the land who could smell and taste a handful of his own earth to find out if the pH was sour or sweet. He cultivated thousands of acres and, as far as I could see, got to have fun all day driving a tractor. I gathered that he had lots of farming knowledge under that hat.

So when I asked him why he always wore it, he took it off and looked at it. He braced his forefinger with a thumb and scratched the top of his head with it. "Keeps the sun off my head," he said.

A good answer, even then. That's just what a gardener's hat does, too. A wide brim keeps rain off the gardener's neck and sun out of the eyes. And because the sun's rays are new and improved under a thinning ozone layer, that's far more important than it used to be. Gardening without a hat these days is courting melanoma.

Joy wears either her straw garden bonnet with its traditional flying-saucer shape or her plum-colored Filson long-billed cap. To say all gardeners wear hats is like saying all accordion players wear rings. There may be exceptions, but not many.

For a time in my life, I lived in the Midwest, in a quiet suburban neighborhood. Across the street lived an elderly Polish woman, small and birdlike, who gardened with lots of mulch and walked with a cane. Her backyard was an orchard, filled with pear, plum, and apple trees. Between the high white pickets of her fence, a rainbow of flowers peeked out. Squash leaves twined underneath, seeking more light and room. Her garden grew up, out, sideways, and down, and outproduced all of her neighbors combined.

Her name, I think, was Mrs. Zybrowski; it was long ago. She couldn't have been a week under ninety-five, but she worked every day of growing season. Atop her tiny head was a woven straw hat the color of a wheat field; it had to be two feet across, a veritable sombrero that cast a big circular shadow on sunny days. The neighborhood kids assumed she was crazy, probably because she shrieked incomprehensibles at them when they vaulted her fence to steal apples. Sometimes she stood on her front porch and pulled up her faded print skirt to moon passing cars, shaking her fist and muttering in squeaky Polish. As far as anyone knew, it was the only language she spoke, other than the green language of plants.

I do not recall ever seeing her at all without that big hat as she spread her mulch. From a distance, it looked like potting soil, and whatever was in it made her flowers explode like nuclear bombs and all her vegetables swell up as if they'd been soaked in gibberellic acid. At harvest time, her relatives, a large and cheerful clan who visited on weekends, carted away bushels of goodies: tomatoes, potatoes, apples and pears, carrots, cucumbers, pumpkins, and horseradish. It made a river of bounty to those she loved, but her neighbors never saw so much as a zucchini.

She ignored all of them, and they ignored her back as hard as they could. Apparently this rift was the result of feuds stretching back for decades and across oceans. I was a new renter on the block, and she snubbed me on general principles all winter, never returning my waves until the day I began to plant a garden in the spring. That April morning, I smiled and waved in a neighborly way, as always, but this time, she didn't turn away. Her whole face contorted, and her beak of a nose bobbed up and down, as if she was making fun of me. At first I thought she was scowling, but I waved again, and then she waved back, with her cane. She was smiling. I realized she wasn't wearing dentures; that was why it looked so much like a snarl.

It might have been my hat that first broke the ice, a slouchy old straw cowboy hat, larger than my childhood version, five gallons or so; not as wide-brimmed as hers, but made of the same straw. Half an hour later, quiet as the rustle of feathers, she appeared on the sidewalk behind me while I was double-digging a bed. I jumped a foot when she spoke. Only a low picket fence separated us.

"Czym uprawiasz swoj ogrod?" she demanded, very loudly.

"Oh, good morning," I replied. No effect. Raising the volume, shrugging, pointing to the sky: "Nice day!"

She shook her head, like an old owl regarding a foolish mouse. Very slowly, enunciating carefully: *"Wodorosty? Popiol? W swoim ogrodzie?"*

"Ah, yes. This is my garden. Yours is quite beautiful. Love your hat."

She muttered what-the-hellski, and tried again. *"Schmutz? Pflanzen? Der Erde?"*

Ah, she also spoke German. I knew a word in German: "Nein."

With a huge sigh, she spread her arms. Back to simple Polish: *"Uzywasz jako kompostu?"*

That one I maybe knew. "My compost? I don't have—"

She cut me off with a cane wave. *"Chlopcze, oddam ci duza przysluge."* She indicated my scraggly garden.

"No, it's not doing so hot," I agreed. "If I spread superphosphate a foot thick, it might—"

"A teraz mlody czlowieku pokaze ci swoja sekretna formule," she announced, snarling toothlessly. She pointed at my wheelbarrow, making waving motions and urging grunts.

Pushing the barrow, hoping that I'd read the signs right, I followed her over to her garden gate. She pointed behind her house, where a chimney was sending up clouds of smoke. An irrational image of Hansel and Gretel intruded into my thoughts. But I followed her anyway.

Inside her yard, I saw a giant wooden bin, compartmentalized into two sections, filled with rich loamy soil: her compost pile. Looking around to see if any of the hated neighbors were nearby, she scuttled into her garage and dragged out a steel garbage can. In the quiet neighborhood, it sounded like Godzilla eating a car. She checked again for neighbors, frowning and swiveling her head. And then took off the lid. A familiar smell hit me, one I hadn't encountered in a long time.

I stared. Of course I recognized the contents, since I'd grown up across the street from the Pacific Ocean. The can was filled with brown hollow bulbs and long smooth flat tentacles, permeated by a fishy smell. "That's kelp," I said softly, but she whipped her finger to her lips. "Kelp," I whispered, thinking she might want to know the English word.

"Kolp?" She giggled, and verbigerated like crazy in Polish, long reeling sentences that were starving for vowels.

Where in the world had she gotten fresh sea kelp in Iowa? It was an anachorism, totally out of place; it was a mystery. It was her secret ingredient.

She pointed to just about every house on the block but mine, pointed to the kelp, and shook her head. By this I understood that none of the bastard neighbors knew, and she wished it to remain so. I put my hand over my heart and winked. You can communicate a lot with gestures. She insisted in mime that I fill the wheelbarrow with compost from her pile; when I diffidently pointed to my wallet, miming an offer to pay for it, she laughed in my face, spouting consonants and gracious little snorts. *"Nein, nein,"* she said.

Over the summer, my garden prospered as never before. The neighbors asked, but I just lied to them. Iowa used to be a seabed, eons ago, and apparently the plants remembered the taste of ancient nutrients, since they thrived on side-dressing with Mrs. Z's Secret Compost Formula: fresh kelp.

Kelp is a remarkable fertilizer, boosting the nutrition value of vegetables as well as their growth. The Japanese have been gardening with kelp for centuries. Full of trace elements, it supplies them to plants in balanced amounts. Carrots grown in seaweed-enriched soil contain more iodine.

But where and how did Mrs. Z get fresh kelp? I never found out, although she probably told me.

There are some things we were not meant to know. There are secrets under every gardener's hat, and some will go to the grave with them. But it's all right to wonder.

I should prefer to grow wiser without growing older.

◆

GEORGE BERNARD SHAW

GRINDSTONE

"How much longer?" This from Serenity, the child we made at home in our spare time, who is now enduring the hell of her thirteenth year. Like most of her questions, it cannot be answered satisfactorily. "Hel-lo-o-o? Dad?"

The problem with this little grindstone is that it is hand-cranked, which presents difficulties when sharpening two-handed tools like a shovel. Someone must be shanghaied and impressed into service as a grindstone apprentice.

"Just a few more minutes." The bevel on a shovel must be steep to make the edge strong; the sharpener who respects the craft of shovel-sharpening must keep the angle constant. It requires focus. These are the very tasks that help gardeners to develop Patience, a most valuable quality for human beings, especially parents, who perhaps can pass this lesson down to their young by osmosis. Telling them is wasted breath.

"Da-ad," Ren lilts, in the weary tone of voice that television has taught all our young to speak, whether they live in Southern California or not. "Dad! Earth to all fathers!"

Kids can bring you out of pleasant reveries the same way that starfish pull a clam from its home, by relentless pressure. "What is it, honey?"

"Are we about, like, done here or what?" She has things to do, places to go, apparently, and zero interest in learning how to hone all these garden tools. She thinks this kind of work is excruciatingly dull.

"Almost. Sorry this is taking so long. I'll finish this shovel and then you can toddle off. Just one more minute. Crank some more, please." She cranks, radiating teen boredom and waves of exasperation. I respond with politeness, retreating into what an old Buddhist teacher called the mantra of America: *Please/sorry/thank*

you. As a tactic, it somewhat disarms the pointed rudeness of youth, and it makes me feel better than arguing.

There is no way to explain to Serenity that adolescence is a time of severe mental agitation, or that it will pass, or even that I recall what it felt like. When she reaches adulthood, she'll probably remember that I kept my tools sharp. Only after she becomes a crone will she understand that I was expounding by example on life's most important lesson: Enjoy whatever you're doing.

"I mean, do we *have* to do this now?" she mutters, not caring if anyone hears or answers. There's no one else from her generation in this shop, no one able to comprehend matters of consequence.

Many gardening books and articles tell you to sharpen your tools after you put them away for the winter. This means, of course, after you collect them from their various locations, clean off the dirt with a hose or wire brush, oil the steel parts and slap linseed on the wood. Autumn, they say, is also the best time to sharpen them.

This is not a lie, but it's not entirely true, either. Those with time on their hands might find it easy. But this cannot possibly mean gardeners, since the post-harvest season is frantic, not to mention that school has started. Those hours spent sharpening a sickle, hoe, shovel, or other garden tool could be better employed canning peas, cleaning beds, tarping the compost, taking down the trellises, planting garlic, or playing basketball. A good compromise is to sharpen a few of the dullest garden tools now, and do the rest next spring.

This little grindstone is a scaled-down shop version of the old farmer's wheel, foot-cranked and water-cooled, that was the family grindstone at the turn of the century. They're collector's items now, but I never got around to collecting one when I saw them at antique stores and farm auctions. Those wheels were sometimes three inches across, a good wide stone that dipped into the water bath with every revolution. They'd edge a shovel in less than a minute.

"It's *been* a minute, Dad. I'd like to have a life today, you know?" Kids helping their parents: No prisoner ever longed for freedom so keenly.

"Go. I'm done, and I really appreciate it. Thank you." She evaporates. I'm not really done, of course. Now the shovel must still be stroked lightly with a file to

hone up a few spots and wiped down with oil. After that, I have a whole pile of tools to sharpen before Monday morning. They may get done, or they may not. It doesn't matter. This is a good way to spend Sunday in meditation, and the profit will not be measured in dollars.

Think of all the people who work on Sunday, all across America. They are nurses, police, teachers, clerks, and firefighters. They are valets and reporters, soldiers and priests, street musicians, ambulance drivers, nurses, and shelter workers. On the first day of the week, when bankers and government workers have their feet up on the hassock, all these people are working a full shift.

Talk to someone with a job they love, if you know anyone like that, and ask them how they feel about working on Sundays. They'll shrug if they don't work or make a face if they do. Welcome to the nineties, where the stores never close and holidays keep the wealth circulating.

There will be no payment forthcoming for sharpening these garden tools, other than inner satisfaction and a sense of accomplishment. The tools used are basic: this little grindstone, a good selection of Nicholson files, a Norton Multi-Stone with three different grades of stone that revolve in an oil bath, and a few stones shaped as cylinders, for running along the edge of a curved blade. For razor edges, I have a ceramic stick and a few leather strops. None of them cost very much, so all of them are paid for. They use no electricity, so they work for free, too.

To sharpen a dull blade, begin by filing or grinding out all the dents and nicks. A wheel tends to make a concave edge, which is where the term "hollow ground" comes from, and it's easy to burn off the temper with an electric grinding wheel. This grindstone is slower but safer. Needless to say, all sharpening operations require gloves and eye protection.

With exceptions, reestablish the original bevel and follow it. That means shovels, hoes, and sickles are sharpened with one bevel, usually the inside edge. The file is brought down toward the edge with steady pressure, lifting the file after each stroke. At the end, one flat stroke is made across the unbeveled back of the tool to remove the wire edge.

The machete and the garden knives have two bevels on their blades, and these must meet at a perfect angle to cut cleanly. This means repetitive stroking along the finest of the three Norton stones, almost sharpening for its own sake.

The hoes are a little trickier. First, I clamp the handles in my shop vise, with a file and whetstone handy to the workbench. The vise, whose miraculous provenance has been described elsewhere, is absolutely the best way to hold a hoe blade steady for sharpening. I've tried squeezing the handles between my legs and filing, but it's discouraging and dangerous when the head suddenly flips over. If you have a shop vise and don't use it for this job, try it once and see for yourself.

Fifteen minutes of filing, a little extra honing with a slipstone, and the Ho-Mi is done. This year, I put a slightly steeper bevel up near the top of the head and filed the point almost flat to make it sharper, which Joy suggested. A gardener we knew complained that his new Ho-Mi was "useless," but it turned out he had never put an edge on it and was trying to use it dull. Loggers around here use the simile "dull as a hoe" to describe dull chainsaws. The phrase goes back at least four generations.

After I'm satisfied with Joy's hoe, I do my own stirrup hoe. It needs a lighter touch on the file because its metal is thinner and more springy, good American steel. When that's done, both hoes go in the five-gallon bucket. After I'm done sharpening all the long tools and no more will fit in the bucket, I'll fill it up with sand and pour in two quarts of motor oil. The sand keeps the steel in contact with the oil, and that way nothing rusts over the winter. In addition, the handles stick up nicely to receive their annual coat of boiled linseed oil. This system of tool storage took many years to evolve, but it works. The sand/oil mix can be reused for years.

I once worked in a stockroom with a man who swore that his soul was damned because he let the system work him "on the one day in the week that has any meaning." A very devout person, he felt the other six days were set aside for sweat of the brow, forty hours of suffering required, but Sunday was a holy day of rest, for prayer and meditation. And here he was working: "violating the Sabbath," he called it. We were stacking boxes in a shipping room.

I saw a solution. "Quit. Get another job where you can stay home and pray on Sunday." It seemed fairly obvious.

He looked at me like a mule looks over a fence on a hot day. "You don't get it. I prayed for this job for three months." He had trouble staying employed (various

addictive disorders), and he knew that God didn't keep that many paying jobs in stock, so he wasn't about to throw away this one. Besides possessing the gift of gratitude, he was an intensely honest human being, and worked hard at being a good man in a world of contradictions.

I told him that, given who he was, coming to work was a service to God and his fellow human beings, since he was sacrificing his set-aside holy day to put bread on the table of his family. He didn't steal from the company, and he didn't loaf. He tithed, 10 percent of his paycheck. "That's prayer of a sort," I said. "Eight full hours of it."

He didn't see it that way. "Prayer," he told me, "is healing. Work grinds you down. Believe me, I know the difference."

Even today, I'm not sure I do. Gibran said that work was love made visible; done in the right spirit, that's exactly what it is. The whole point of work-as-service is to expend energy making the world a better place, to heal the planet in any small way possible, and to work mindfully, without losing sight of your soul.

Long ago, I asked the universe for a livelihood that would keep me interested, humble, and permanently learning. It didn't have to be highly paid; just enough to meet our simple needs. Working Sundays would be okay, I added. Now I work Sundays, and holidays, too. Every day, in fact.

Working in the garden and woodworking define my life, and writing about it pays the bills. The odd part is, writing is largely a way of figuring out the relationship of this life to gardening and carpentry. Like any other job, you start with what you have in the way of marketable skills, learn your weaknesses, hide them or overcome them, and go in search of employment. Some days you sail, and some days you slog. Some days, it's easier to write than others.

It's also a way to explain things so I can understand them. Until now, I've never really examined the process of putting a keen edge on a garden tool.

The trick in sharpening a lot of tools is to go slowly, and to sharpen each individual tool without thinking about the last one or the next one. The shovel doesn't need to be very sharp, so I can use a grindstone and file, but the machete must have a razor edge. That means working the steel with a whetstone, followed by a few strokes on a leather strop. I've spent three hours sharpening a machete to get just the right edge. Ren would call that a waste of time; and in fact, she has.

The sickle's blade needs a steady rest and stroking with a slipstone, which is a round whetstone held in the hand and slipped along the edge. Irregular blades like this don't clamp very well, so I have to brace it on the workbench.

Finally, I'm almost done. Sunday flows around me like a river, a day of peace and restoration, and it looks like there might be time enough for a brief nap before I go to work at my keyboard. But just as I'm putting all the newly sharp tools away, Ren returns, proclaiming a minor emergency. "Dad, we've got to go to town. I need a whole bunch of stuff for school tomorrow."

A number of critical-parent responses cycle through my mind: Why didn't you mention this earlier? What makes a trip to town so imperative? Do you think I've got nothing better to do than etcetera and so on? But this is where putting a keen edge on my own attention pays off. I'm now sharp enough to see that the whole point of this Sunday is maintaining harmony and peace, and performing service to those I love with a smile. So I smile. "Okay. Give me a minute to get ready, and I'll drive you in."

If you know how to do one thing well, you can do everything.

✦

GURDJIEFF

RAKE

"In this world, there are easy things and hard things. Do the hard jobs first or last, whatever you choose. But do them without fail." It was my third-grade teacher, Ms. Hydinger, who imparted this seminal lesson in the nature of life, and it seems so simple, but this advice has been acquiring more meaning with the passage of years. It's about character in the face of obstacles.

Getting raked over the coals should be put off as long as possible, even forever, in my humble opinion. But here it is, the end of fall already. Since the family is visiting far-off relatives and won't have to witness the event, this might be a good day to quit smoking. To assist, I have prescription patches the size of coasters, a bottle of homeopathic pills, thirty feet of licorice, several good affirmations, and a will of iron. Deliberately, I seize this moment to strike off the shackles of nicotine.

Twenty-four hours glide by like a slug traveling over broken glass. There's an amusing little short story by Kafka called "The Harrow." If you've never smoked, read it sometime to get the sense of what quitting feels like. By nightfall, I eat everything in the refrigerator but the ice. A paper sign is held to the door by magnetic walnut shells: GRATITUDE IS THE PROPER ATTITUDE. Another goddamn affirmation; Joy put it there, and I can't imagine what she was thinking.

At midnight, I eat the ice, sucking cubes to simulate menthol. For hours, I sit on the verge of some sweeping internal discovery, a revelation of such power and glory that my mind hesitates to reveal it all at once, but finally it does: *You need cigarettes. You should go to town and buy them.*

These are the most insidious thoughts. No one in the world understands your problems like the Lady Nicotine. And you are out of licorice. And you do feel sorry for yourself. Why not throw the dog a bone? Just one cigarette. One puff.

No. *Vade retro me*, you suck-sticks.

Therefore, the next day's sun rises on a whimpering maniac: unfocused, unshaven, scratching a patch over his heart, a man who can't finish sentences or concentrate on anything except just one more hit of tobacco, forever postponed. An alien face looks back from the mirror, sallow as the belly of a dead catfish, complete with limp barbels and peeling scales.

Coffee is not a good idea because it makes the urge to break something feel as natural as breathing air flavored with smoke. By itself, oxygen is a tasteless, odorless, boring gas.

Only two more days of hell and then I can work on the psychological part of the addiction. Nicotine is not a subtle drug. Quitting is no more painful than being flayed and staked out on an anthill. Everything in life is suddenly defined by my senses. I can see perfectly for thousands of yards down the hill: a cigarette cocked merrily in the lips of a tourist cruising on the highway. The colorful pack peeks out of his shirt pocket, and his smile is as big and curved as an elephant's bung. Is it imagination, or can I smell the smoke from here? Easily.

Food has taken on consummate importance. Already before noon, I've consumed the whole nine yards of licorice rope, snapping it up like a shark eating transatlantic phone cable. It should get easier this time, the very last time, as soon as my hands stop shaking with the urge to strangle myself.

Out in the shop, I'm so clumsy that I drop a mayonnaise jar full of nails, in an almost-but-not-quite unconscious search for the mythical Lost Cigarette Butt. It explodes on the concrete floor: a lovely shattering sound, harmonically attuned to the human nervous system, as soothing and moving as a cigarette.

I'm drowning in self-pity when my brother, Jonathan, drops by on his motorcycle. He pats me on the back while I claw at my chest, and then he listens to the usual tirade: my passionate hatred for an industry that turned a Native American sacrament into just another addiction; my fervent wish to see festering boils on the faces of those who serve them in Congress; and a big dose of leprosy for their chemists who boost the jones factor. Jon nods in the right places, and he has a lot of compassion. But no pity.

"Yeah, that's all true. They're real scumbags, and you're not going to pay them any more money. Listen, you're doing fine. Three days and you're over the hump. Take it an hour at a time, and if you absolutely need a cigarette, call me first before you light it." Jon is an ex-smoker with mountains of willpower, who quit by visualizing his family at his own funeral. "Remember, this is the best thing you can do for your health, your family, and your self-respect. Anyway, the reason I came, apart from moral support, was to ask a favor . . ."

My ears aren't translating anything into English. I have a hard time concentrating, but it finally becomes clear: Jon wants some help designing a short, lightweight rake with a T-handle. "For Melinda," he explains. Melinda is his girlfriend.

This is something I did not know. Melinda gardens?

"Sure. Wheelchair gardens are real common; didn't you know that? But if you're disabled, you have to do some planning first.

"It's like this: You put your individual shrubs in front, right up next to the hard surface, concrete or whatever. You put those in raised beds so they're accessible. No plant should be taller than two feet, so you can still reach it, and the beds should be no wider than five feet. And all the row crops like radishes and carrots go in back," he says evenly, "so you can crawl to them."

That blows me away. That's dedicated gardening.

Since meeting Melinda, Jon has learned things about disability that few able persons would suspect, and now he notices stairs and parking places. There are places that wheelchairs can't go, but gardens shouldn't be one of them. "She can't shovel, obviously, but a rake is a good gardening tool. She just needs something a lot lighter. You should see her run a scratch weeder under her tomato plants. Can you make her a rake?" I say yes. It will take a few days, though, because I'm twisting on the spit right now. Jon just smiles, the way all ex-smokers smile.

"Don't give up," he says, putting on his helmet. "Never give up."

After that visit, I go out to our garden and rake aimlessly in a patch of dirt, not really trying to accomplish anything except keeping my hands busy making smooth lines, and thinking about rake design. Jon has a way of putting things in perspective: I have a minor problem with drug withdrawal, that's all. I'm grateful he stopped by. Two more days and the nicotine will be flushed out. Compared to the lifelong challenges some people must face, mine are insignificant. So much for self-pity.

A rake is a good tool for inducing calm. A teenager raking leaves, a monk raking designs into pebbles in a Zen garden, a gardener raking the fresh-tilled earth: These are images of peace. Why that should be, I'm not sure. For some reason, raking is synonymous with silence and relaxation.

And it is relaxing. In the spring, after the tiller has done its work, Joy and I start shaping the beds. First, we rake out all the debris cast up by the tiller: hard clumps of dirt or sod, root balls, last year's stems, tree roots, and all the other compost fodder goes in the wheelbarrow. We use the rake with the shovel to pile up the beds, pulling the earth off the paths and combing it out flat at the same time. Soon our garden is a patchwork of clearly defined squares and rectangles, with a few triangular beds rounding it out. In a morning or afternoon, all the beds are raked smooth and flat, and the work flows along without struggle.

You can get quite fond of a good rake. My favorite garden rake has no identifiers, no patents stamped in the head or stickers on the handle, so I imagine it was made by hand. It's super-heavy-duty, of course. The handle is thicker and longer than a standard rake handle, almost seven feet, and the head itself looks like it came from a blacksmith's shop, many years ago. It must weigh at least two pounds. We also have a lighter thatching rake, with dozens of sharp blades instead of tines, and its function is to loosen up the thatch on our lawn. Using that rake is less of a picnic than the others, though, because it tears its way through the turf. By contrast, the bamboo leaf rake easily gathers up anything the trees drop, and this big garden rake does everything else.

For years, I've called raking "horticultural therapy," but it turns out there really is a job description called horticultural therapist, and even an American Horticultural Therapy Association. Gardens have always been considered highly therapeutic for everybody, but the spiritual benefits for the disabled are off the scale, improving feelings of independence, lifting depression, and getting people anchored in an empowering hobby. Horticultural therapy is not a new science, but it's well organized now. After both world wars, veterans' hospitals and volunteers worked together to design user-friendly gardens for recovering warriors. Surgery patients healed faster; trauma patients had time to get their bearings.

Part of the job of horticultural therapists today is designing gardens that can be used by anyone: ambulatory, sighted, or otherwise. For accessibility, garden gates should be three feet wide and slide-by rather than swinging. For wheelchair users, ramps need to be three feet wide and edged to prevent the chair from rolling off. Wheelchair gardeners can tend fairly large plots if there are wooden or concrete surfaces to work from. Benches and wide patios for wheelchair parking need to be strategically located throughout the garden, and well shaded. Raised beds allow the handicapped gardener to reach plants, and if possible, they should be built with extra-wide tops so a disabled person can sit on them. They should be just wide enough so that every plant is in easy reach, and solidly built.

One registered horticultural therapist, Gene Rothert, wrote a wonderful book on handicapped gardening in 1994 called *The Enabling Garden*. It is a comprehensive work, covering not only those who use wheelchairs but any gardener whose mobility is impaired by arthritis, illness, blindness, or age. He recommends that herbs and wildflowers be planted, to attract bees, butterflies, and hummingbirds, to make the garden a more natural environment. Mr. Rothert uses a wheelchair, so he writes from experience.

I'm still trying to think of ways to build this rake for Jon, and in the back of my mind is an impression that I've seen one before, but I can't quite remember where. A cigarette would help me focus. I rake a little longer, purposely not concentrating on anything, and it comes. It must have been about five years ago.

Got it. I was on a bus going through a Boston suburb when I saw a man raking his garden from a wheelchair. It was just a quick glimpse. The handle of that rake seemed to be shorter than average, and something else was odd about it. I have seen rakes operated in every possible way, and thought I knew about every kind of rake, but this new wrinkle raised all sorts of questions. What was the rest of his garden like? After a minute of debate, I pulled the cord and got off, walking back the other way.

But I couldn't find him again, and all the houses looked exactly alike. After an hour of looking, I found a bus stop and resumed my escape from Boston. I didn't stop wondering about that rake. The head seemed to be made of wood.

Lack of nicotine not only hones the senses but the imagination. I've been picturing how delicious it would be to smoke a cigarette, and it's an incredibly vivid fantasy. But what would it be like to garden from a wheelchair? This comes into focus just as clearly. One would have to follow the hard lawn's edge, careful not to let the

wheels sink in where the flower beds begin. Our garden slants downhill at a ten-degree angle and the terrain is too bumpy, so crawling would be the best option.

Yet another reason to be grateful: the heretofore unnoticed power of ambulation. It makes gardening a lot easier.

There are two main kinds of rakes: light lawn rakes and heavy-duty garden rakes. Lawn rakes, which are lighter and are used with a sweeping motion, only work for gathering up leaves and grass clippings for garden mulch. The raker uses a sweeping action, brushing the leaves into piles and then into bags.

However, show a teenager a leaf blower and the rake will be flung aside. They're faster and easier, but they have nothing to do with the concepts of peace or silence, and in some municipalities, leaf blowers are outlawed or the hours of operation are limited. A two-cycle engine makes an ungodly racket.

Garden rakes are heavier, for pulling all the tiller debris out of the soil and smoothing out beds. This type of rake leaves a beautifully striated track, its tines sifting the loose soil in a restful back-and-forth motion, throw and drag.

What is badly needed is a third kind of rake, one that can be operated with a single hand, and preferably while seated. As far as I know, it does not exist. If there were a third kind of rake, one which was a hybrid of the first two, it would combine the lightness of the first with the function of the second: ideal for handicapped gardeners.

One of the things such a rake should have—let's call it a wheelchair rake, for want of a better name—is a special handle. At first, I think in terms of a T-handle or a D-handle at the end, but then I find the Get-a-Grip handle attachment in the Earthmade catalog, and it suits perfectly. It was designed as an ergonomic attachment for tools such as hoes and rakes, made to clamp on a perpendicular to the handle, like the nibs on a scythe. Placed near the end, it will make the three-foot handle a lot easier to hold. That, I finally remember, was the anomalous detail about that rake in Boston: it had a perpendicular handle extension.

I decide to make the head out of spruce, which is light and strong: a sixteen-inch piece for the head, with a row of rounded oak dowels spaced evenly, and the handle socketed and well braced. All rakes used to be made out of wood, anyway, so there should be some books on making a wooden rake in the library. The handle could also be spruce, or possibly good quality aluminum tubing. Aircraft-grade tubing wouldn't be too expensive, considering how much stronger it would be. Strong and light and lovely to hold in your hand . . .

Speaking of nicotine, the third morning is a little better, but still hard. When left on all night, nicotine patches induce shocking, full-color dreams.

Day three is the pinnacle of desire, a time when I'd sell my soul for one cigarette and make change. It seems like as good a time as any to start on the rake, but while cleaning the workbench, I come across half a cigarette. It is probably two months old, and rats have had their way with it; but a kind of tunnel vision constricts everything in the universe down to those delicious spotted two inches.

Crumbling this disgusting thing up and throwing it away is a real challenge. But not a *real* challenge, the kind many people must face every day. For which I'm tremendously grateful.

All things are difficult before they are easy.

◆

THOMAS FULLER

GARDEN KNIFE

The Cutting Edge

Oct.ber is one of those thoughtful months. It's not quite time to put the garden to bed, but the sunflowers have had it. Reaching high, I decapitate them with a machete and gently put their seedy heads in the basket. Another chop at the base, and eight feet of stem joins the other long, woody debris headed for the compost. By bundling them and chopping them on a stump, I can chip them up in wholesale lots, letting the pieces fall in another basket. A shredder would speed this process, but the machete is quieter.

To my mind, it's just a big garden knife, a tool for cutting rough brush or harvesting pumpkins. Today, I'll try to chop out the blackberry empire that has begun to encroach on the southern end of our garden. It's pointless; nothing can beat a blackberry patch. Their roots go right down to magma; tornadoes steer around them to save wind. You can chop blackberry vines to pieces, burn the site, plant salt with a curse, and run a flood through it, but come next spring, it looks as healthy as ever, thrusting forth blue-black berries the size of your thumb.

This patch has been growing patiently uphill for decades, knowing that someday I'll go away, and then it can take the house and suck it under. All over the meadows of Oregon, barn-sized clumps of blackberries cast their thorny tentacles to the sky. Napalm, bulldozers, and machetes are equally futile, but the last is good exercise, and I can eat berries while I work. It's an excellent place to think.

By way of occupational therapy tools, I own four machetes, each with its own merits. One is a military surplus machete, very springy steel, with an olive-drab rubber sheath, designed to last an entire war. I don't use it in the garden, but it's a good camping tool. My second version is a heftier and longer cane-cutter's machete, whose provenance is odd: supposedly it was smuggled from Cuba, along with a box of Cuban cigars, the only tobacco product that is illegal in the United States. The third knife is a smoke-eater's machete, issued to fire-line crews in the Forestry Service. It has a sawblade on the back edge, and a cunning L-shaped red plastic handle.

But my favorite machete, the one I'll use today, is the Woodman's Pal, a wicked-looking stubby machete with a brush hook at the tip. (For those interested, I found it accidentally on the Internet at www.woodmanspal.com and so can you. Also, a few garden catalogs carry them.) Originally developed for jungle warfare in World War II, this machete came back to the States with returning warriors, one of whom was my father. He put a Pal in my hand when I was eleven and taught me how to clear brush with it. Of course I lost it. When I bought one this year, I hadn't touched a Pal in thirty-five years.

October is also the month of Joy's birth, and at first, I didn't have a clue what to get her. But I remembered that she didn't have a really good garden knife, and had been using scissors instead. If the gardener in your life has everything, ask if they have a gardening knife. They will probably say yes and no, since many gardeners have a knife of some sort that gets used in the garden. It may be an old pocketknife, or a worn-down butcher knife, or a Japanese soil knife, or in Joy's case, an old folding linoleum knife. Let's call it that, since ranchers use the same type of knife for castrating calves.

In the Walt Nicke catalog, I found the perfect gift: a folding garden knife made in England, with a Sheffield stainless-steel hawkbill blade, a leather hanging thong, and a bright orange handle of indestructible plastic. It was designed for the garden, and a new version has a humped grip on the blade for those who wear gloves.

After collecting the penny that superstition demands, I gave it to her, and just in time for harvest season. It's even better than a machete for cutting zucchini, squash, and pumpkin stems, but it may not seem like an indispensable garden tool until spring, when you must cut tough nylon string and garden cloth with your partner's scissors or a dull castrating knife. Any pair of sewing scissors found in a garden caddy has been used to cut small twigs and stems; you can bet everything down to your pocket change on that. If it's not rusty, it's dirty, and it's probably so dull that it won't cut nylon string, cord, or baling twine. Good garden shears will, but they're not designed to cut garden cloth or separate a squash from its stem, as knives are.

The first pruning tool was a knife, not a shears. In fact, it wasn't until this century that the shears finally took over; prior to that, arborists and landscapers valued a sharp knife that made mirror-smooth cuts because the stem healed faster. A knife is still the best tool, if not the only tool, for budding and grafting.

One of my earliest memories of watching a garden knife in use is seen dimly, through a rime-frosted window I was licking at the time. Outside, a man stood in a foot of snow, trimming a pear tree with a pocketknife and letting the branches fall in the snow. I can recall the back of his heavy coat, shoulders dusted with snow. Whoever this man was—he could have been my grandfather—he seemed to know exactly what he was doing. He walked around the tree several times before he started. What possessed adults to attack a tree and cut off its branches was far beyond me, but why anyone would do it in the dead of winter struck me as weird even then.

As in carpentry, the trick to getting straight lines in a garden is to use string. This means driving two stakes at opposite ends of a bed and stretching a nylon line between them, to make an easy guide for planting seeds. For small patches of carrots or radishes, you can drag a Warren hoe or a Ho-Mi down the bed, and that's close enough. But for planting corn or other row crops, do yourself a favor: Follow a string-line. Otherwise, your corn rows will wander all over and be difficult to cultivate, as my first year's crop was.

String is a simple tool. There are only two ways to go wrong using braided string in the garden, and having discovered them, I'll share. First, do not cut braided string when it's taut; six feet of it will come unraveled. Pinch a loop between finger and thumb and cut there. Second, do not attempt to run a tiller along a string to create a straight furrow, since the tiller will inevitably catch on the string, slurp it up around its tines, and maybe the engine will die. Then you'll have to cut it all loose from the tines, with only a valuable lesson to show for it.

The first and last time I tangled the Mantis with string, I cut some of it loose with Joy's old U-shaped hoe knife, but for the really tightly wound Gordian knots, a garden knife was the only solution.

It shines in a lot of garden-specific tasks, but for clearing vines, it's too small. A machete may seem like a fairly brutal tool for gardening, but the strip between the herbage and the sown should be kept weed-free. Barbed tentacles are always reaching under the fence, seeking a grip on our garden's throat. If not for frequent machete attention, the southeast corner would succumb to the jungle.

After a few minutes of chopping vines, I start to think about my father, who taught me how to whittle with a pocketknife and how to use a machete. He was born

TOOLS OF THE EARTH

in October, in 1926. To the rest of the world, he was an ordinary man, one of the millions of vets who came back from the war to go to work. He became a reporter and editor for small newspapers in the Midwest, but it was not until I saw him cutting a coconut with a machete on television that I understood: My father had some remarkable skills. He had been invited to chop the thick husk off a green coconut in front of a studio audience, whack a hole in the top, and pour a drink of coconut milk for the show's host. He made it look easy.

He's gone now, but I see his face in the mirror when I shave. Mac gave me my first pocketknife, and my first machete. My hands now resemble his; I first noticed his hands the day he showed me the proper grip for cutting with a machete, paying attention to the way he closed them over mine.

"Squeeze the grip tight; lock your fist. Be careful on the backswing, and bring the blade down at an angle. Keep your shoulder loose. Let the weight do the cutting." Soon after, I was hacking down blackberry vines like a pro, while he told me about Guam, Saipan, Tinian, and the other islands he had visited during the war. His tools included a similar machete with a finger-guard, like a stubby saber, and a Thompson .45 submachine gun. He was in the Marianas from 1943 to 1945, and those jungles had marked him with interesting scars.

There's a bench down here, in a briar-enclosed glade between the house and the river, under the shade of a maple tree. We came down here one last time, the summer before Mac got sick. His diagnosis had been confirmed, and he said he wanted to visit this place once more. That hot day, his shirt was off, and I noticed the old scar over one rib, a puckered crater whose bottom touched the bone. Always before, he had brushed off questions about this particular war wound, saying only that it was from a Japanese pistol. I asked him again.

After a time, he said, "There were two Marines, way out in the boonies, and they were—bothering a Chamorran girl, she must have been about fifteen. I asked them to knock it off. They didn't, so I put the Thompson on them and *told* them to stop. One of them whipped out a souvenir Nambu; he got off a round."

"They *shot* you?"

"I was a Fleet Marine. Different animal altogether." He shrugged. "The powder was old, or wet, and the slug bounced off. It knocked the wind out of me, but their pants were still around their ankles.

"Anyway, they stopped."

The machete's saber-edge pares away the thorny vines until the base of the clump is exposed, and whack! it's gone, flush with the soil. The roots are dug in, ten feet down. They're patient.

Part of the blackberry patch is sacred. On his deathbed, my father asked me to leave it untouched down by the river where it meets the tall sedge grass at the edge of the forest, as a habitat for rabbits, the Green Man's domain, a place reserved for the spirits of the jungle. He was quite reverent about that place, which he called "the wildwood," and claimed he had seen things in there he had not encountered since the jungles of Guam, fifty years ago. I don't go there with a machete in my hands.

The true art of memory is the art of attention.

◆

SAMUEL JOHNSON

HARVEST BASKET
The Answers of Autumn

Harvest time means hours spent gathering fruit, but they are truly timeless; no one keeps track of time spent in a garden. Joy and I have already done this stoop labor for hours without denting the ripe tomatoes popping out like measles across the green face of our garden: Early Girl, Willamette, Oregon Spring, Little Boy, Fat Man, and Tomato Glut. I planted too many. The seed catalog seduced me. It's going to be dark soon. I'm curious: "When are we going to stop doing tomatoes, honey?"

Ask a silly question, get a silly smile from Joy. Night approaches, with the sun sliding down the few centimeters above the western hills, but a little daylight remains. "If you remember," she says, "someone said we couldn't *possibly* have too many tomatoes. So that's how many we planted." What a fantastic memory she has. That's what I said, verbatim. It was true then, but apparently it's not now. You *can* have too many tomatoes.

And now, with our kitchen buried in tomatoes, our counter crimson with tomatoes, and the pressure cooker oozing love-applesauce around the clock, I finally understand the concept of infinity squared and other imaginary numbers. Picking and processing tomatoes was great fun for the first two days, when we were fresh. Now it reminds me of school, when the hours dripped like ketchup from the bottle and all eyes were glued to the clock. If they wanted us to learn about time and numbers, they should have sent us to the country to pick fruit.

In the early part of a child's life, he or she will be forced to do elementary arithmetical problems based on originally agriculture units of measurement: acres, barrels, buckets, bushels, pecks, and so forth. This baby student will at no time be shown an actual acre of land, a peck basket, a tin bucket, or a real wooden barrel, nor will a realtime bushel of produce ever find its way into the classroom. Instead, they will get symbols. Pictures of bushels are drawn with corn heaped high, for visual recognition, but the likely result is a confused kid. A level bushel

is 32 quarts, and all kids have seen a quart of milk, so the little tykes must try to figure it out from there.

When my Uncle Bob first showed me a bushel basket, my first reaction was awe, followed by a rising anger. I had been cheated by the educational system. In the first place, this bushel was not filled to the top and never would be, since, as my uncle explained, corn would spill out of it when it was moved. Take out a handful of corn, or add one, or leave it alone, and it was still a bushel of corn: a big margin of error. In the second place, there was *no such thing* as a thousand bushels in physical reality—despite the fact that I had been forced to do numerous equations with that measurement. Quite simply, a thousand bushels is how much corn goes in a silo—and it is not measured with a thousand bushel baskets or one basket filled a thousand times. However, thanks to my uncle, I finally understood the concept by extrapolating from this actual bushel.

During twelve years in the juvenile gulag, I had never seen one bushel full of shelled corn. There it was, missing all this time, the single thing needed to grasp "bushel" as a *Ding-an-sich*. When I asked him how much an acre was, he showed me; it had a tree on it for scale, and 1.5 horses, the smaller unit nursing from the larger. My uncle had no teaching certificate because they don't give them out to the self-educated, but he knew how to answer a simple question. As a teacher and a farmer, he was out standing in his field.

The earliest American settlers made their own garden tools and implements. They wove strips of steamed wood to make baskets, and this became part of the craft of making "treenware," common utensils carved or woven from wood. You can read all about this in any of Eric Sloane's excellent books, particularly *A Reverence for Wood*, illustrated with his superb drawings. Making your own harvest baskets and trugs is not out of the question, if you have time and like to putter.

Another tomato plops in the trug. We have filled it many times; "many" is more than a lot, but less than enough. A bushel basket of tomatoes yields a bottom layer of mashed tomato sauce about yea-thick, so the wise gardener instead collects them in the traditional English trug.

Something close to the trug design was used by many Native American tribes, a flat woven basket for gathering roots and berries, often decorated with expensive art: priceless, in fact. You can see them in museums.

More affordable trugs can be had through catalogs, in Walt Nicke's just to name one. They range in price from twenty to sixty dollars, and in size from one pint to four gallons. The history of the English trug begins in East Sussex, where they have been made by hand for 150 years. Thick strips of chestnut are split, shaped with a drawknife, and heated in a steamer until they're pliable enough to wrap around a form. Split willow makes a rim, another piece makes the handle, and everything is fixed together with copper nails.

They look a little like small boats, which were once called "trogs"; hence the name. Queen Victoria, that practical empress, ordered a big batch as soon as she saw them, and the maker delivered them in a wheelbarrow, sixty miles on foot. That's the weird kind of dedication and pride you should look for in any garden tool supplier.

Long ago, a trug held exactly two-thirds of a bushel, but this measurement is so obsolete that it's no longer taught. (I was almost forty before even I heard the word "trug," losing at Scrabble to an expert.) These days, a trug is just a flat rectangular basket made of wood or super-duper plastic, designed to keep fragile fruit from being stacked too high. It holds as much as a small raccoon weighs, and it's as long as a piece of string. A trug of any size always contains one trug's worth of garden bounty.

Anyway, I have my answer from Joy: the time remaining is an unknown quantity. We will have to pick tomatoes until none are left, or we get tired, or it gets too dark to see.

Like fishing, the garden is one place where measurements can mean whatever you want them to mean. Problems of any kind do not exist in gardens; all you have to do is think differently and they vanish. In gardens, challenges certainly can multiply at an exponential rate, and ditto learning experiences, but a problem cannot simultaneously occupy head-space filled with peace. If you wish, scrape the math off your boots like mud and concentrate on the variables of experience.

The geometry of our garden is such a complicated universe that I don't even try to comprehend it. Joy talks to the plant devas and flower fairies to figure out where everything should go, what cultivars and how many, and then she consults the moon for a timetable, holds her green thumb to the wind, and away we go. I plod along behind, taking notes.

The corn equation was much simplified by raccoons, who deducted so much corn that we had a fighting chance of getting the remainder husked, cobbed, and frozen. In my ignorance, despite Joy's advice, I planted five long rows of Startling Abundance and Yellow Hernia, east to west so they'd self-pollinate, and they did. Thank God for the little masked footpads. What the coons left was still an abundant harvest, too many bushels. At one point, shucking corn, I prayed they'd come back that night and take the rest. They didn't touch the zucchini; raccoons are discriminating thieves.

Ren is inside doing her homework, but only in theory. She's probably on the phone with her best friend. The ratio of hours spent on homework to hours spent discussing fine boys and harsh parental guidelines is probably unequal, but we approve of this multitasking because education is a holistic ideal. It will be all right if she knows the primary export of Bolivia, but even better if she learns how to communicate with her peers. Her math teacher, obviously a genius, started the year with a cross-discipline sermon on the importance of reading, and books as the building blocks of all learning. Inspired, Ren came home and began with Stephen King. Her math grades immediately improved. Whatever they're paying this educator, it isn't enough.

Our apple tree tripled its output this year, giving us four times as many apples as we needed. We fed some to the horse at the ratio of three per horse per day, and it still left us with one bushel, one gunnysack, two boxes, and a rubber bucket of apples, which are still piled among the green and red tomatoes in our kitchen. How many of each? The number is the least important thing about them. They are red. They may be Brandywines.

The first evening star has begun to twinkle when Joy speaks: "Okay, I'm tired. Had enough? Ready for supper?"

To tell the truth, I was done fifteen minutes ago. Next year, I'll plan our tomatoes better, meaning fewer and with staggered harvests. Heaving up our trugs, we go inside to grab a bite, make some coffee, and stoke up the pressure cooker and food dryer. The night is young, and we have hours of canning to go.

Knowledge comes, but wisdom lingers.

✦

TENNYSON